The Noble Eightfold Path

The Noble Eightfold Path

Way to the End of Suffering

Bhikkhu Bodhi

BPS PARIYATTI EDITIONS

BPS Pariyatti Editions

AN IMPRINT OF
Pariyatti Publishing
www.pariyatti.org

Published with the consent of the original publisher.
Copies of this book for sale in the Americas only.

First BPS Pariyatti Edition, 2000

Print ISBN: 978-1-681722-93-1
PDF ISBN: 978-1-928706-82-3
ePub ISBN: 978-1-928706-81-6
Mobi ISBN: 978-1-928706-83-0
LCCN: 00057182

Library of Congress Cataloging-in-Publication Data
Bodhi, Bhikkhu.
  The noble eightfold path : way to the end of suffering / Bhikkhu Bodhi.
    p. cm.

  Includes bibliographical references.
  ISBN 1-928706-07-X (pbk.)
    1. Buddhism.

BQ4320 .B63 2000
4.3'444--dc21

00-057182

Contents

ABOUT THE AUTHOR

Bhikkhu Bodhi is an American Buddhist monk, born and raised in New York City. Ordained as a monk in Sri Lanka in 1972, he lived in Sri Lanka for over twenty years, where he was president and editor of the Buddhist Publication Society. He now resides at Bodhi Monastery in rural New Jersey. He is the co-translator of *The Middle Length Discourses of the Buddha* (Majjhima Nikāya) and translator of *The Connected Discourses of the Buddha* (Saṃyutta Nikāya). His most recent work is *In the Buddha's Words.*

PREFACE

The essence of the Buddha's teaching can be summed up in two principles: the Four Noble Truths and the Noble Eightfold Path. The first covers the side of doctrine, and the primary response it elicits is understanding; the second covers the side of discipline, in the broadest sense of that word, and the primary response it calls for is practice. In the structure of the teaching these two principles lock together into an indivisible unity called the dhamma-vinaya, the doctrine-and-discipline, or, in brief, the Dhamma. The internal unity of the Dhamma is guaranteed by the fact that the last of the Four Noble Truths, the truth of the way, is the Noble Eightfold Path, while the first factor of the Noble Eightfold Path, right view, is the understanding of the Four Noble Truths. Thus the two principles penetrate and include one another, the formula of the Four Noble Truths containing the Eightfold Path and the Noble Eightfold Path containing the Four Truths.

Given this integral unity, it would be pointless to pose the question which of the two aspects of the Dhamma has greater value, the doctrine or the path. But if we did risk the pointless by asking that question, the answer would have to be the path. The path claims primacy because it is precisely this that brings the teaching to life. The path translates the Dhamma from a collection of abstract formulas into a continually unfolding disclosure of truth. It gives an outlet from the problem of suffering with which the teaching starts. And it makes the teaching's goal, liberation from suffering, accessible to us in our own experience, where alone it takes on authentic meaning.

To follow the Noble Eightfold Path is a matter of practice rather than intellectual knowledge, but to apply the path correctly it has to be properly understood. In fact, right understanding of the path is itself a part of the practice. It is a facet of right view, the first path factor, the forerunner and guide for the rest of the path. Thus, though initial enthusiasm might suggest that the task of intellectual comprehension may be shelved as a bothersome distraction, mature consideration reveals it to be quite essential to ultimate success in the practice.

The present book aims at contributing towards a proper understanding of the Noble Eightfold Path by investigating its eight factors and their components to determine exactly what they involve. I have attempted to be concise, using as the framework for exposition the Buddha's own words in explanation of the path factors, as found in the Sutta Piṭaka of the Pāli Canon. To assist the reader with limited access to primary sources even in translation, I have tried to confine my selection of quotations as much as possible (but not completely) to those found in Venerable Nyanatiloka's classic anthology, The Word of the Buddha. In some cases passages taken from that work have been slightly modified, to accord with my own preferred renderings. For further amplification of meaning I have sometimes drawn upon the commentaries; especially in my accounts of concentration and wisdom (Chapters VII and VIII) I have relied heavily on the Visuddhimagga (The Path of Purification), a vast encyclopedic work which systematizes the practice of the path in a detailed and comprehensive manner. Limitations of space prevent an exhaustive treatment of each factor. To compensate for this deficiency I have included a list of recommended readings at the end, which the reader may consult for more detailed explanations of individual path factors. For full commitment to the practice of the path, however, especially in its advanced stages of concentration and insight, it will be extremely helpful to have contact with a properly qualified teacher.

Bhikkhu Bodhi

ABBREVIATIONS

Textual references have been abbreviated as follows:

DN	=	Dīgha Nikāya (number of sutta)
MN	=	Majjhima Nikāya (number of sutta)
SN	=	Saṃyutta Nikāya (chapter and number of sutta)
AN	=	Aṅguttara Nikāya (numerical collection and number of sutta)
Dhp	=	Dhammapada (verse)
Vism	=	Visuddhimagga

References to Vism. are to the chapter and section number of the translation by Bhikkhu Ñāṇamoli, The Path of Purification (BPS ed. 1975, 1991, 1999; BPE ed. 1999).

THE WAY TO THE END
OF SUFFERING

The search for a spiritual path is born out of suffering. It does not start with lights and ecstasy, but with the hard tacks of pain, disappointment, and confusion. However, for suffering to give birth to a genuine spiritual search, it must amount to more than something passively received from without. It has to trigger an inner realization, a perception which pierces through the facile complacency of our usual encounter with the world to glimpse the insecurity perpetually gaping underfoot. When this insight dawns, even if only momentarily, it can precipitate a profound personal crisis. It overturns accustomed goals and values, mocks our routine preoccupations, leaves old enjoyments stubbornly unsatisfying.

At first such changes generally are not welcome. We try to deny our vision and to smother our doubts; we struggle to drive away the discontent with new pursuits. But the flame of inquiry, once lit, continues to burn, and if we do not let ourselves be swept away by superficial readjustments or slouch back into a patched up version of our natural optimism, eventually the original glimmering of insight will again flare up, again confront us with our essential plight. It is precisely at that point, with all escape routes blocked, that we are ready to seek a way to bring our disquietude to an end. No longer can we continue to drift complacently through life, driven blindly by our hunger for sense pleasures and by the pressure of prevailing social norms. A deeper reality beckons us; we have heard the call of a more stable, more authentic happiness, and until we arrive at our destination we cannot rest content.

But it is just then that we find ourselves facing a new difficulty. Once we come to recognize the need for a spiritual path we discover that spiritual teachings are by no means homogeneous and mutually compatible. When we browse through the shelves of humanity's spiritual heritage, both ancient and contemporary, we do not find a single tidy volume but a veritable bazaar of spiritual systems and disciplines each offering themselves to us as the highest, the fastest, the most powerful, or the most profound solution to our quest for the Ultimate. Confronted with this melange, we fall into confusion trying to size them up—to decide which is truly liberative, a real solution to our needs, and which is a sidetrack beset with hidden flaws.

One approach to resolving this problem that is popular today is the eclectic one: to pick and choose from the various traditions whatever seems amenable to our needs, welding together different practices and techniques into a synthetic whole that is personally satisfying. Thus one may combine Buddhist mindfulness meditation with sessions of Hindu mantra recitation, Christian prayer with Sufi dancing, Jewish Kabbala with Tibetan visualization exercises. Eclecticism, however, though sometimes helpful in making a transition from a predominantly worldly and materialistic way of life to one that takes on a spiritual hue, eventually wears thin. While it makes a comfortable halfway house, it is not comfortable as a final vehicle.

There are two interrelated flaws in eclecticism that account for its ultimate inadequacy. One is that eclecticism compromises the very traditions it draws upon. The great spiritual traditions themselves do not propose their disciplines as independent techniques that may be excised from their setting and freely recombined to enhance the felt quality of our lives. They present them, rather, as parts of an integral whole, of a coherent vision regarding the fundamental nature of reality and the final goal of the spiritual quest. A spiritual tradition is not a shallow stream in which one can wet one's feet and then beat a quick retreat to the shore. It is a mighty, tumultuous river which would rush through the entire landscape of one's life, and if one truly wishes to travel on it, one must be courageous enough to launch one's boat and head out for the depths.

The second defect in eclecticism follows from the first. As spiritual practices are built upon visions regarding the nature of reality and the final good, these visions are not mutually compatible.

When we honestly examine the teachings of these traditions, we will find that major differences in perspective reveal themselves to our sight, differences which cannot be easily dismissed as alternative ways of saying the same thing. Rather, they point to very different experiences constituting the supreme goal and the path that must be trodden to reach that goal.

Hence, because of the differences in perspectives and practices that the different spiritual traditions propose, once we decide that we have outgrown eclecticism and feel that we are ready to make a serious commitment to one particular path, we find ourselves confronted with the challenge of choosing a path that will lead us to true enlightenment and liberation. One cue to resolving this dilemma is to clarify to ourselves our fundamental aim, to determine what we seek in a genuinely liberative path. If we reflect carefully, it will become clear that the prime requirement is a way to the end of suffering. All problems ultimately can be reduced to the problem of suffering; thus what we need is a way that will end this problem finally and completely. Both these qualifying words are important. The path has to lead to a *complete* end of suffering, to an end of suffering in all its forms, and to a *final* end of suffering, to bring suffering to an irreversible stop.

But here we run up against another question. How are we to find such a path—a path which has the capacity to lead us to the full and final end of suffering? Until we actually follow a path to its goal we cannot know with certainty where it leads, and in order to follow a path to its goal we must place complete trust in the efficacy of the path. The pursuit of a spiritual path is not like selecting a new suit of clothes. To select a new suit one need only try on a number of suits, inspect oneself in the mirror, and select the suit in which one appears most attractive. The choice of a spiritual path is closer to marriage: one wants a partner for life, one whose companionship will prove as trustworthy and durable as the pole star in the night sky.

Faced with this new dilemma, we may think that we have reached a dead end and conclude that we have nothing to guide us but personal inclination, if not a flip of the coin. However, our selection need not be as blind and uninformed as we imagine, for we do have a guideline to help us. Since spiritual paths are generally presented in the framework of a total teaching, we can evaluate the effectiveness of any particular path by investigating the teaching which expounds it.

In making this investigation we can look to three criteria as standards for evaluation:

(1) *First,* the teaching has to give a full and accurate picture of the range of suffering. If the picture of suffering it gives is incomplete or defective, then the path it sets forth will most likely be flawed, unable to yield a satisfactory solution. Just as an ailing patient needs a doctor who can make a full and correct diagnosis of his illness, so in seeking release from suffering we need a teaching that presents a reliable account of our condition.

(2) The *second* criterion calls for a correct analysis of the causes giving rise to suffering. The teaching cannot stop with a survey of the outward symptoms. It has to penetrate beneath the symptoms to the level of causes, and to describe those causes accurately. If a teaching makes a faulty causal analysis, there is little likelihood that its treatment will succeed.

(3) The *third* criterion pertains directly to the path itself. It stipulates that the path which the teaching offers has to remove suffering at its source. This means it must provide a method to cut off suffering by eradicating its causes. If it fails to bring about this root-level solution, its value is ultimately nil. The path it prescribes might help to remove symptoms and make us feel that all is well; but one afflicted with a fatal disease cannot afford to settle for cosmetic surgery when below the surface the cause of his malady continues to thrive.

To sum up, we find three requirements for a teaching proposing to offer a true path to the end of suffering: first, it has to set forth a full and accurate picture of the range of suffering; second, it must present a correct analysis of the causes of suffering; and third, it must give us the means to eradicate the causes of suffering.

This is not the place to evaluate the various spiritual disciplines in terms of these criteria. Our concern is only with the Dhamma, the teaching of the Buddha, and with the solution this teaching offers to the problem of suffering. That the teaching should be relevant to this problem is evident from its very nature; for it is formulated, not as a set of doctrines about the origin and end of things commanding belief, but as a message of deliverance from suffering claiming to be verifiable in our own experience. Along with that message there comes a method of practice, a way leading to the end of suffering. This way is the Noble Eightfold Path (*ariya aṭṭhaṅgika magga*). The Eightfold Path stands at the very heart of the Buddha's teaching. It was the discovery of the path that gave the Buddha's own enlightenment a universal significance and elevated him from the status of a wise and benevolent sage to that of a world teacher. To his own disciples he was pre-eminently "the arouser of the path unarisen before, the producer of the path not produced before, the declarer of the path not declared before, the knower of the path, the seer of the path, the guide along the path" (MN 108). And he himself invites the seeker with the promise and challenge: "You yourselves must strive. The Buddhas are only teachers. The meditative ones who practise the path are released from the bonds of evil" (Dhp. v. 276).

To see the Noble Eightfold Path as a viable vehicle to liberation, we have to check it out against our three criteria: to look at the Buddha's account of the range of suffering, his analysis of its causes, and the programme he offers as a remedy.

The Range of Suffering

The Buddha does not merely touch the problem of suffering tangentially; he makes it, rather, the very cornerstone of his teaching. He starts the Four Noble Truths that sum up his message with the announcement that life is inseparably tied to something he calls *dukkha*. The Pāli word is often translated as suffering, but it means something deeper than pain and misery. It refers to a basic unsatisfactoriness running through our lives, the lives of all but the enlightened. Sometimes this unsatisfactoriness erupts into the open as sorrow, grief, disappointment, or despair; but usually it hovers at the edge of our awareness as a vague unlocalized sense that things are never quite perfect, never fully adequate to our expectations of what they should be. This fact of *dukkha,* the Buddha says, is the only real spiritual problem. The other problems—the theological and metaphysical questions that have taunted religious thinkers through the centuries—he gently waves aside as "matters not tending to liberation." What he teaches, he says, is just suffering and the ending of suffering, *dukkha* and its cessation.

The Buddha does not stop with generalities. He goes on to expose the different forms that *dukkha* takes, both the evident and the subtle. He starts with what is close at hand, with the suffering inherent in the physical process of life itself. Here *dukkha* shows up in the events of birth, aging, and death, in our susceptibility to sickness, accidents, and injuries, even in hunger and thirst. It appears again in our inner reactions to disagreeable situations and events: in the sorrow, anger, frustration, and fear aroused by painful separations, by unpleasant encounters, by the failure to get what we want. Even our pleasures, the Buddha says, are not immune from *dukkha*. They give us happiness while they last, but they do not last forever; eventually they must pass away, and when they go the loss leaves us feeling deprived. Our lives, for the most part, are strung out between the thirst for pleasure and the fear of pain. We pass our days running after the one and running away from the other, seldom enjoying the peace of contentment; real satisfaction seems somehow always out of reach, just beyond the next horizon. Then in the end we have to die: to give up the identity we spent our whole life building, to leave behind everything and everyone we love.

But even death, the Buddha teaches, does not bring us to the end of *dukkha,* for the life process does not stop with death. When life ends in one place, with one body, the "mental continuum," the individual stream of consciousness, springs up again elsewhere with a new body as its physical support. Thus the cycle goes on over and over—birth, aging, and death—driven by the thirst for more existence. The Buddha declares that this round of rebirths—called *saṃsāra,* "the wandering"—has been turning through beginningless time. It is without a first point, without temporal origin. No matter how far back in time we go we always find living beings—ourselves in previous lives—wandering from one state of existence to another. The Buddha describes various realms where rebirth can take place: realms of torment, the animal realm, the human realm, realms of celestial bliss. But none of these realms can offer a final refuge. Life in any plane must come to an end. It is impermanent and thus marked with that insecurity which is the deepest meaning of *dukkha*. For this reason one aspiring to the complete end of *dukkha* cannot rest content with any mundane achievement, with any status, but must win emancipation from the entire unstable whirl.

The Causes of Suffering

A teaching proposing to lead to the end of suffering must, as we said, give a reliable account of its causal origination. For if we want to put a stop to suffering, we have to stop it where it begins, with its causes. To stop the causes requires a thorough knowledge of what they are and how they work; thus the Buddha devotes a sizeable section of his teaching to laying bare "the truth of the origin of *dukkha*." The origin he locates within ourselves, in a fundamental malady that permeates our being, causing disorder in our own minds and vitiating our relationships with others and with the world. The sign of this malady can be seen in our proclivity to certain unwholesome mental states called in Pāli *kilesas,* usually translated "defilements." The most basic defilements are the triad of greed, aversion, and delusion. Greed (*lobha*) is self-centered desire: the desire for pleasure and possessions, the drive for survival, the urge to bolster the sense of ego with power, status, and prestige. Aversion (*dosa*) signifies the response of negation, expressed as rejection, irritation, condemnation, hatred, enmity, anger, and violence. Delusion (*moha*) means mental darkness: the thick coat of insensitivity which blocks out clear understanding.

From these three roots emerge the various other defilements—conceit, jealousy, ambition, lethargy, arrogance, and the rest—and from all these defilements together, the roots and the branches, comes *dukkha* in its diverse forms: as pain and sorrow, as fear and discontent, as the aimless drifting through the round of birth and death. To gain freedom from suffering, therefore, we have to eliminate the defilements. But the work of removing the defilements has to proceed in a methodical way. It cannot be accomplished simply by an act of will, by wanting them to go away. The work must be guided by investigation. We have to find out what the defilements depend upon and then see how it lies within our power to remove their support.

The Buddha teaches that there is one defilement which gives rise to all the others, one root which holds them all in place. This root is ignorance (*avijjā*).[1] Ignorance is not mere absence of knowledge, a lack of knowing particular pieces of information. Ignorance can co-exist with a vast accumulation of itemized knowledge, and in its own way it can be tremendously shrewd and resourceful. As the basic root of *dukkha*, ignorance is a fundamental darkness shrouding the mind. Sometimes this ignorance operates in a passive manner, merely obscuring correct understanding. At other times it takes on an active role: it becomes the great deceiver, conjuring up a mass of distorted perceptions and conceptions which the mind grasps as attributes of the world, unaware that they are its own deluded constructs.

In these erroneous perceptions and ideas we find the soil that nurtures the defilements. The mind catches sight of some possibility of pleasure, accepts it at face value, and the result is greed. Our hunger for gratification is thwarted, obstacles appear, and up spring anger and aversion. Or we struggle over ambiguities, our sight clouds, and we become lost in delusion. With this we discover the breeding ground of *dukkha*: ignorance issuing in the defilements, the defilements issuing in suffering. As long as this causal matrix stands we are not yet beyond danger. We might still find pleasure and enjoyment—sense pleasures, social pleasures, pleasures of the mind and heart. But no matter how much pleasure we might experience, no matter how successful we might be at dodging pain, the basic problem remains at the core of our being and we continue to move within the bounds of *dukkha*.

Cutting Off the Causes of Suffering

To free ourselves from suffering fully and finally we have to eliminate it by the root, and that means to eliminate ignorance. But how does one go about eliminating ignorance? The answer follows clearly from the nature of the adversary. Since ignorance is a state of not knowing things as they really are, what is needed is knowledge of things as they really are. Not merely conceptual knowledge, knowledge as idea, but perceptual knowledge, a knowing which is also a seeing. This kind of knowing is called wisdom (*paññā*). Wisdom helps to correct the distorting work of ignorance. It enables us to grasp things as they are in actuality, directly and immediately, free from the screen of ideas, views, and assumptions our minds ordinarily set up between themselves and the real.

To eliminate ignorance we need wisdom, but how is wisdom to be acquired? As indubitable knowledge of the ultimate nature of things, wisdom cannot be gained by mere learning, by gathering and accumulating a battery of facts. However, the Buddha says, wisdom can be cultivated. It comes into being through a set of conditions, conditions which we have the power to develop. These conditions are actually mental factors, components of consciousness, which fit together into a systematic structure that can be called a path in the word's essential meaning: a courseway for movement leading to a goal. The goal here is the end of suffering, and the path leading to it is the Noble Eightfold Path with its eight factors: right view, right intention, right speech, right action, right livelihood, right effort, right mindfulness, and right concentration.

The Buddha calls this path the middle way (*majjhimā paṭipadā*). It is the middle way because it steers clear of two extremes, two misguided attempts to gain release from suffering. One is the extreme of indulgence in sense pleasures, the attempt to extinguish dissatisfaction by gratifying desire. This approach gives pleasure, but the enjoyment won is gross, transitory, and devoid of deep contentment. The Buddha recognized that sensual desire can exercise a tight grip over the minds of human beings, and he was keenly aware of how ardently attached people become to the pleasures of the senses. But he also knew that this pleasure is far inferior to the happiness that arises from renunciation, and therefore he repeatedly taught that the way to the Ultimate eventually requires the relinquishment of sensual desire. Thus the Buddha describes the indulgence in sense pleasures as "low, common, worldly, ignoble, not leading to the goal."

The other extreme is the practice of self-mortification, the attempt to gain liberation by afflicting the body. This approach may stem from a genuine aspiration for deliverance, but it works within the compass of a wrong assumption that renders the energy expended barren of results. The error is taking the body to be the cause of bondage, when the real source of trouble lies in the mind—the mind obsessed by greed, aversion, and delusion. To rid the mind of these defilements the affliction of the body is not only useless but self-defeating, for it is the impairment of a necessary instrument. Thus the Buddha describes this second extreme as "painful, ignoble, not leading to the goal."[2]

Aloof from these two extreme approaches is the Noble Eightfold Path, called the middle way, not in the sense that it effects a compromise between the extremes, but in the sense that it transcends them both by avoiding the errors that each involves. The path avoids the extreme of sense indulgence by its recognition of the futility of desire and its stress on renunciation. Desire and sensuality, far from being means to happiness, are springs of suffering to be abandoned as the requisite of deliverance. But the practice of renunciation does not entail the tormenting of the body. It consists in mental training, and for this the body must be fit, a sturdy support for the inward work. Thus the body is to be looked after well, kept in good health, while the mental faculties are trained to generate the liberating wisdom. That is the middle way, the Noble Eightfold Path, which "gives rise to vision, gives rise to knowledge, and leads to peace, to direct knowledge, to enlightenment, to Nibbāna."[3]

II

RIGHT VIEW
(Sammā Diṭṭhi)

The eight factors of the Noble Eightfold Path are not steps to be followed in sequence, one after another. They can be more aptly described as components rather than as steps, comparable to the intertwining strands of a single cable that requires the contributions of all the strands for maximum strength. With a certain degree of progress all eight factors can be present simultaneously, each supporting the others. However, until that point is reached, some sequence in the unfolding of the path is inevitable. Considered from the standpoint of practical training, the eight path factors divide into three groups: (i) the moral discipline group (sīlakkhandha), made up of right speech, right action, and right livelihood; (ii) the concentration group (samādhikkhandha), made up of right effort, right mindfulness, and right concentration; and (iii) the wisdom group (paññākkhandha), made up of right view and right intention. These three groups represent three stages of training: the training in the higher moral discipline, the training in the higher consciousness, and the training in the higher wisdom.[1]

The order of the three trainings is determined by the overall aim and direction of the path. Since the final goal to which the path leads, liberation from suffering, depends ultimately on uprooting ignorance, the climax of the path must be the training directly opposed to ignorance. This is the training in wisdom, designed to awaken the faculty of penetrative understanding which sees things "as they really are." Wisdom unfolds by degrees, but even the faintest flashes of insight presuppose as their basis a mind that has been concentrated, cleared of disturbance and distraction. Concentration is achieved through the training in the higher consciousness, the second division of the path, which brings the calm and collectedness needed to develop wisdom. But in order for the mind to be unified in concentration, a check must be placed on the unwholesome dispositions which ordinarily dominate its workings, since these dispositions disperse the beam of attention and scatter it among a multitude of concerns. The unwholesome dispositions continue to rule as long as they are permitted to gain expression through the channels of body and speech as bodily and verbal deeds. Therefore, at the very outset of training, it is necessary to restrain the faculties of action, to prevent them from becoming tools of the defilements. This task is accomplished by the first division of the path, the training in moral discipline. Thus the path evolves through its three stages, with moral discipline as the foundation for concentration, concentration the foundation for wisdom, and wisdom the direct instrument for reaching liberation.

Perplexity sometimes arises over an apparent inconsistency in the arrangement of the path factors and the threefold training. Wisdom—which includes right view and right intention—is the last stage in the threefold training, yet its factors are placed at the beginning of the path rather than at its end, as might be expected according to the canon of strict consistency. The sequence of the path factors, however, is not the result of a careless slip, but is determined by an important logistical consideration, namely, that right view and right intention of a preliminary type are called for at the outset as the spur for entering the threefold training. Right view provides the perspective for practice, right intention the sense of direction. But the two do not expire in this preparatory role. For when the mind has been refined by the training in moral discipline and concentration, it arrives at a superior right view and right intention, which now form the proper training in the higher wisdom.

Right view is the forerunner of the entire path, the guide for all the other factors. It enables us to understand our starting point, our destination, and the successive landmarks to pass as practice advances. To attempt to engage in the practice without a foundation of right view is to risk getting lost in the futility of undirected movement. Doing so might be compared to wanting to drive someplace without consulting a roadmap or listening to the suggestions of an experienced driver. One might get into the car and start to drive, but rather than approaching closer to one's destination, one is more likely to move farther away from it. To arrive at the desired place one has to have some idea of its general direction and of the roads leading to it. Analogous considerations apply to the practice of the path, which takes place in a framework of understanding established by right view.

The importance of right view can be gauged from the fact that our perspectives on the crucial issues of reality and value have a bearing that goes beyond mere theoretical convictions. They govern our attitudes, our actions, our whole orientation to existence. Our views might not be clearly formulated in our mind; we might have only a hazy conceptual grasp of our beliefs. But whether formulated or not, expressed or maintained in silence, these views have a far-reaching influence. They structure our perceptions, order our values, crystallize into the ideational framework through which we interpret to ourselves the meaning of our being in the world.

These views then condition action. They lie behind our choices and goals, and our efforts to turn these goals from ideals into actuality. The actions themselves might determine consequences, but the actions along with their consequences hinge on the views from which they spring. Since views imply an "ontological commitment," a decision on the question of what is real and true, it follows that views divide into two classes, right views and wrong views. The former correspond to what is real, the latter deviate from the real and confirm the false in its place. These two different kinds of views, the Buddha teaches, lead to radically disparate lines of action, and thence to opposite results. If we hold a wrong view, even if that view is vague, it will lead us towards courses of action that eventuate in suffering. On the other hand, if we adopt a right view, that view will steer us towards right action, and thereby towards freedom from suffering. Though our conceptual orientation towards the world might seem innocuous and inconsequential, when looked at closely it reveals itself to be the decisive determinant of our whole course of future development. The Buddha himself says that he sees no single factor so responsible for the arising of unwholesome states of mind as wrong view, and no factor so helpful for the arising of wholesome states of mind as right view. Again, he says that there is no single factor so responsible for the suffering of living beings as wrong view, and no factor so potent in promoting the good of living beings as right view (AN 1:16.2).

In its fullest measure right view involves a correct understanding of the entire Dhamma or teaching of the Buddha, and thus its scope is equal to the range of the Dhamma itself. But for practical purposes two kinds of right view stand out as primary. One is mundane right view, right view which operates within the confines of the world. The other is supramundane right view, the superior right view which leads to liberation from the world. The first is concerned with the laws governing material and spiritual progress within the round of becoming, with the principles that lead to higher and lower states of existence, to mundane happiness and suffering. The second is concerned with the principles essential to liberation. It does not aim merely at spiritual progress from life to life, but at emancipation from the cycle of recurring lives and deaths.

Mundane Right View

Mundane right view involves a correct grasp of the law of *kamma,* the moral efficacy of action. Its literal name is "right view of the ownership of action" (*kammassakatā sammādiṭṭhi*), and it finds its standard formulation in the statement: "Beings are the owners of their actions, the heirs of their actions; they spring from their actions, are bound to their actions, and are supported by their actions. Whatever deeds they do, good or bad, of those they shall be heirs."[2] More specific formulations have also come down in the texts. One stock passage, for example, affirms that virtuous actions such as giving and offering alms have moral significance, that good and bad deeds produce corresponding fruits, that one has a duty to serve mother and father, that there is rebirth and a world beyond the visible one, and that religious teachers of high attainment can be found who expound the truth about the world on the basis of their own superior realization.[3]

To understand the implications of this form of right view we first have to examine the meaning of its key term, *kamma.* The word *kamma* means action. For Buddhism the relevant kind of action is volitional action, deeds expressive of morally determinate volition, since it is volition that gives the action ethical significance. Thus the Buddha expressly identifies action with volition. In a discourse on the analysis of *kamma* he says: "Monks, it is volition that I call action (*kamma*). Having willed, one performs an action through body, speech, or mind."[4] The identification of *kamma* with volition makes *kamma* essentially a mental event, a factor originating in the mind which seeks to actualize the mind's drives, dispositions, and purposes. Volition comes into being through any of three channels—body, speech, or mind—called the three doors of action (*kammadvāra*). A volition expressed through the body is a bodily action; a volition expressed through speech is a verbal action; and a volition that issues in thoughts, plans, ideas, and other mental states without gaining outer expression is a mental action. Thus the one factor of volition differentiates into three types of *kamma* according to the channel through which it becomes manifest.

Right view requires more than a simple knowledge of the general meaning of *kamma*. It is also necessary to understand: (i) the ethical distinction of *kamma* into the unwholesome and the wholesome; (ii) the principal cases of each type; and (iii) the roots from which these actions spring. As expressed in a sutta: "When a noble disciple understands what is kammically unwholesome, and the root of unwholesome *kamma*, what is kammically wholesome, and the root of wholesome *kamma*, then he has right view."[5]

(i) Taking these points in order, we find that *kamma* is first distinguished as unwholesome (*akusala*) and wholesome (*kusala*). Unwholesome *kamma* is action that is morally blameworthy, detrimental to spiritual development, and conducive to suffering for oneself and others. Wholesome *kamma*, on the other hand, is action that is morally commendable, helpful to spiritual growth, and productive of benefits for oneself and others.

(ii) Innumerable instances of unwholesome and wholesome *kamma* can be cited, but the Buddha selects ten of each as primary. These he calls the ten courses of unwholesome and wholesome action. Among the ten in the two sets, three are bodily, four are verbal, and three are mental. The ten courses of unwholesome *kamma* may be listed as follows, divided by way of their doors of expression:

The ten courses of wholesome *kamma* are the opposites of these: abstaining from the first seven courses of unwholesome *kamma*, being free from covetousness and ill will, and holding right view. Though the seven cases of abstinence are exercised entirely by the mind and do not necessarily entail overt action, they are still designated wholesome bodily and verbal action because they centre on the control of the faculties of body and speech.

1. Destroying life
2. Taking what is not given
3. Wrong conduct in regard to
   sense pleasures

} Bodily action
(*kāyakamma*)

4. False speech
5. Slanderous speech
6. Harsh speech
7. Idle chatter

} Verbal action
(*vacikamma*)

8. Covetousness
9. Ill will
10. Wrong view

} Mental action
(*manokamma*)

(iii) Actions are distinguished as wholesome and unwholesome on the basis of their underlying motives, called "roots" (*mūla*), which impart their moral quality to the volitions concomitant with themselves. Thus *kamma* is wholesome or unwholesome according to whether its roots are wholesome or unwholesome. The roots are threefold for each set. The unwholesome roots are the three defilements we already mentioned—greed, aversion, and delusion. Any action originating from these is an unwholesome *kamma*. The three wholesome roots are their opposites, expressed negatively in the old Indian fashion as non-greed (*alobha*), non-aversion (*adosa*), and non-delusion (*amoha*). Though these are negatively designated, they signify not merely the absence of defilements but the corresponding virtues. Non-greed implies renunciation, detachment, and generosity; non-aversion implies loving-kindness, sympathy, and gentleness; and non-delusion implies wisdom. Any action originating from these roots is a wholesome *kamma*.

The most important feature of *kamma* is its capacity to produce results corresponding to the ethical quality of the action. An immanent universal law holds sway over volitional actions, bringing it about that these actions issue in retributive consequences, called *vipāka*, "ripenings," or *phala*, "fruits." The law connecting actions with their fruits works on the simple principle that unwholesome actions ripen in suffering, wholesome actions in happiness. The ripening need not come right away; it need not come in the present life at all. *Kamma* can operate across the succession of lifetimes; it can even remain dormant for aeons into the future. But whenever we perform a volitional action, the volition leaves its imprint on the mental continuum, where it remains as a stored up potency. When the stored up *kamma* meets with conditions favourable to its maturation, it awakens from its dormant state and triggers off some effect that brings due compensation for the original action. The ripening may take place in the present life, in the next life, or in some life subsequent to the next. A *kamma* may ripen by producing rebirth into the next existence, thus determining the basic form of life; or it may ripen in the course of a lifetime, issuing in our varied experiences of happiness and pain, success and failure, progress and decline. But whenever it ripens and in whatever way, the same principle invariably holds: wholesome actions yield favourable results, unwholesome actions yield unfavourable results.

To recognize this principle is to hold right view of the mundane kind. This view at once excludes the multiple forms of wrong view with which it is incompatible. As it affirms that our actions have an influence on our destiny continuing into future lives, it opposes the nihilistic view which regards this life as our only existence and holds that consciousness terminates with death. As it grounds the distinction between good and evil, right and wrong, in an objective universal principle, it opposes the ethical subjectivism which asserts that good and evil are only postulations of personal opinion or means to social control. As it affirms that people can choose their actions freely, within limits set by their conditions, it opposes the "hard deterministic" line that our choices are always made subject to necessitation, and hence that free volition is unreal and moral responsibility untenable.

Some of the implications of the Buddha's teaching on the right view of *kamma* and its fruits run counter to popular trends in present-day thought, and it is helpful to make these differences explicit. The teaching on right view makes it known that good and bad, right and wrong, transcend conventional opinions about what is good and bad, what is right and wrong. An entire society may be predicated upon a confusion of correct moral values, and even though everyone within that society may applaud one particular kind of action as right and condemn another kind as wrong, this does not make them validly right and wrong. For the Buddha moral standards are objective and invariable. While the moral character of deeds is doubtlessly conditioned by the circumstances under which they are performed, there are objective criteria of morality against which any action, or any comprehensive moral code, can be evaluated. This objective standard of morality is integral to the Dhamma, the cosmic law of truth and righteousness. Its transpersonal ground of validation is the fact that deeds, as expressions of the volitions that engender them, produce consequences for the agent, and that the correlations between deeds and their consequences are intrinsic to the volitions themselves. There is no divine judge standing above the cosmic process who assigns rewards and punishments. Nevertheless, the deeds themselves, through their inherent moral or immoral nature, generate the appropriate results.

For most people, the vast majority, the right view of *kamma* and its results is held out of confidence, accepted on faith from an eminent spiritual teacher who proclaims the moral efficacy of action. But even when the principle of *kamma* is not personally seen, it still remains a facet of right view. It is part and parcel of right view because right view is concerned with understanding—with understanding our place in the total scheme of things—and one who accepts the principle that our volitional actions possess a moral potency has, to that extent, grasped an important fact pertaining to the nature of our existence. However, the right view of the kammic efficacy of action need not remain exclusively an article of belief screened behind an impenetrable barrier. It can become a matter of direct seeing. Through the attainment of certain states of deep concentration it is possible to develop a special faculty called the "divine eye" (*dibbacakkhu*), a super-sensory power of vision that reveals things hidden from the eyes of flesh. When this faculty is developed, it can be directed out upon the world of living beings to investigate the workings of the kammic law. With the special vision it confers one can then see for oneself, with immediate perception, how beings pass away and re-arise according to their *kamma,* how they meet happiness and suffering through the maturation of their good and evil deeds.[6]

Superior Right View

The right view of *kamma* and its fruits provides a rationale for engaging in wholesome actions and attaining high status within the round of rebirths, but by itself it does not lead to liberation. It is possible for someone to accept the law of *kamma* yet still limit his aims to mundane achievements. One's motive for performing noble deeds might be the accumulation of meritorious *kamma* leading to prosperity and success here and now, a fortunate rebirth as a human being, or the enjoyment of celestial bliss in the heavenly worlds. There is nothing within the logic of kammic causality to impel the urge to transcend the cycle of *kamma* and its fruit. The impulse to deliverance from the entire round of becoming depends upon the acquisition of a different and deeper perspective, one which yields insight into the inherent defectiveness of all forms of saṃsāric existence, even the most exalted.

This superior right view leading to liberation is the understanding of the Four Noble Truths. It is this right view that figures as the first factor of the Noble Eightfold Path in the proper sense: as the *noble* right view. Thus the Buddha defines the path factor of right view expressly in terms of the four truths: "What now is right view? It is understanding of suffering (*dukkha*), understanding of the origin of suffering, understanding of the cessation of suffering, understanding of the way leading to the cessation of suffering."[7] The Eightfold Path starts with a conceptual understanding of the Four Noble Truths apprehended only obscurely through the media of thought and reflection. It reaches its climax in a direct intuition of those same truths, penetrated with a clarity tantamount to enlightenment. Thus it can be said that the right view of the Four Noble Truths forms both the beginning and the culmination of the way to the end of suffering.

The first noble truth is the truth of suffering (*dukkha*), the inherent unsatisfactoriness of existence, revealed in the impermanence, pain, and perpetual incompleteness intrinsic to all forms of life.

> This is the noble truth of suffering. Birth is suffering; aging is suffering; sickness is suffering; death is suffering; sorrow, lamentation, pain, grief, and despair are suffering; association with the unpleasant is suffering; separation from the pleasant is suffering; not to get what one wants is suffering; in brief, the five aggregates of clinging are suffering.[8]

The last statement makes a comprehensive claim that calls for some attention. The five aggregates of clinging (*pañcupādānak-kandhā*) are a classificatory scheme for understanding the nature of our being. What we are, the Buddha teaches, is a set of five aggregates—material form, feelings, perceptions, mental formations, and consciousness—all connected with clinging. We are the five and the five are us. Whatever we identify with, whatever we hold to as our self, falls within the set of five aggregates. Together these five aggregates generate the whole array of thoughts, emotions, ideas, and dispositions in which we dwell, "our world." Thus the Buddha's declaration that the five aggregates are *dukkha* in effect brings all experience, our entire existence, into the range of *dukkha*.

But here the question arises: Why should the Buddha say that the five aggregates are *dukkha*? The reason he says that the five aggregates are *dukkha* is that they are impermanent. They change from moment to moment, arise and fall away, without anything substantial behind them persisting through the change. Since the constituent factors of our being are always changing, utterly devoid of a permanent core, there is nothing we can cling to in them as a basis for security. There is only a constantly disintegrating flux which, when clung to in the desire for permanence, brings a plunge into suffering.

The second noble truth points out the cause of *dukkha*. From the set of defilements which eventuate in suffering, the Buddha singles out craving (*taṇhā*) as the dominant and most pervasive cause, "the origin of suffering."

> This is the noble truth of the origin of suffering. It is this craving which produces repeated existence, is bound up with delight and lust, and seeks pleasure here and there, namely, craving for sense pleasures, craving for existence, and craving for non-existence.[9]

The third noble truth simply reverses this relationship of origination. If craving is the cause of *dukkha*, then to be free from *dukkha* we have to eliminate craving. Thus the Buddha says:

> This is the noble truth of the cessation of suffering. It is the complete fading away and cessation of this craving, its forsaking and abandonment, liberation and detachment from it.[10]

The state of perfect peace that comes when craving is eliminated is Nibbāna (*nirvāṇa*), the unconditioned state experienced while alive with the extinguishing of the flames of greed, aversion, and delusion. The fourth noble truth shows the way to reach the end of *dukkha*, the way to the realization of Nibbāna. That way is the Noble Eightfold Path itself.

The right view of the Four Noble Truths develops in two stages. The first is called the right view that accords with the truths (*saccānulomika sammā diṭṭhi*); the second, the right view that penetrates the truths (*saccapaṭivedha sammā diṭṭhi*). To acquire the right view that accords with the truths requires a clear understanding of their meaning and significance in our lives. Such an understanding arises first by learning the truths and studying them. Subsequently it is deepened by reflecting upon them in the light of experience until one gains a strong conviction as to their veracity.

But even at this point the truths have not been penetrated, and thus the understanding achieved is still defective, a matter of concept rather than perception. To arrive at the experiential realization of the truths it is necessary to take up the practice of meditation—first to strengthen the capacity for sustained concentration, then to develop insight. Insight arises by contemplating the five aggregates, the factors of existence, in order to discern their real characteristics. At the climax of such contemplation the mental eye turns away from the conditioned phenomena comprised in the aggregates and shifts its focus to the unconditioned state, Nibbāna, which becomes accessible through the deepened faculty of insight. With this shift, when the mind's eye sees Nibbāna, there takes place a simultaneous penetration of all Four Noble Truths. By seeing Nibbāna, the state beyond *dukkha*, one gains a perspective from which to view the five aggregates and see that they are *dukkha* simply because they are conditioned, subject to ceaseless change. At the same moment Nibbāna is realized, craving stops; the understanding then dawns that craving is the true origin of *dukkha*. When Nibbāna is seen, it is realized to be the state of peace, free from the turmoil of becoming. And because this experience has been reached by practising the Noble Eightfold Path, one knows for oneself that the Noble Eightfold Path is truly the way to the end of *dukkha*.

This right view that penetrates the Four Noble Truths comes at the end of the path, not at the beginning. We have to start with the right view conforming to the truths, acquired through learning and fortified through reflection. This view inspires us to take up the practice, to embark on the threefold training in moral discipline, concentration, and wisdom. When the training matures, the eye of wisdom opens by itself, penetrating the truths and freeing the mind from bondage.

III

RIGHT INTENTION
(Sammā Saṅkappa)

The second factor of the path is called in Pāli *sammā saṅkappa,* which we will translate as "right intention." The term is sometimes translated as "right thought," a rendering that can be accepted if we add the proviso that in the present context the word "thought" refers specifically to the purposive or conative aspect of mental activity, the cognitive aspect being covered by the first factor, right view. It would be artificial, however, to insist too strongly on the division between these two functions. From the Buddhist perspective, the cognitive and purposive sides of the mind do not remain isolated in separate compartments but intertwine and interact in close correlation. Emotional predilections influence views, and views determine predilections. Thus a penetrating view of the nature of existence, gained through deep reflection and validated through investigation, brings with it a restructuring of values which sets the mind moving towards goals commensurate with the new vision. The application of mind needed to achieve those goals is what is meant by right intention.

The Buddha explains right intention as threefold: the intention of renunciation, the intention of good will, and the intention of harmlessness.[1] The three are opposed to three parallel kinds of wrong intention: intention governed by desire, intention governed by ill will, and intention governed by harmfulness.[2] Each kind of right intention counters the corresponding kind of wrong intention. The intention of renunciation counters the intention of desire, the intention of good will counters the intention of ill will, and the intention of harmlessness counters the intention of harmfulness.

The Buddha discovered this twofold division of thought in the period prior to his Enlightenment (see MN 19). While he was striving for deliverance, meditating in the forest, he found that his thoughts could be distributed into two different classes. In one he put thoughts of desire, ill will, and harmfulness, in the other thoughts of renunciation, good will, and harmlessness. Whenever he noticed thoughts of the first kind arise in him, he understood that those thoughts lead to harm for oneself and others, obstruct wisdom, and lead away from Nibbāna. Reflecting in this way he expelled such thoughts from his mind and brought them to an end. But whenever thoughts of the second kind arose, he understood those thoughts to be beneficial, conducive to the growth of wisdom, aids to the attainment of Nibbāna. Thus he strengthened those thoughts and brought them to completion.

Right intention claims the second place in the path, between right view and the triad of moral factors that begins with right speech, because the mind's intentional function forms the crucial link connecting our cognitive perspective with our modes of active engagement in the world. On the one side actions always point back to the thoughts from which they spring. Thought is the forerunner of action, directing body and speech, stirring them into activity, using them as its instruments for expressing its aims and ideals. These aims and ideals, our intentions, in turn point back a further step to the prevailing views. When wrong views prevail, the outcome is wrong intention giving rise to unwholesome actions. Thus one who denies the moral efficacy of action and measures achievement in terms of gain and status will aspire to nothing but gain and status, using whatever means he can to acquire them. When such pursuits become widespread, the result is suffering, the tremendous suffering of individuals, social groups, and nations out to gain wealth, position, and power without regard for consequences. The cause for the endless competition, conflict, injustice, and oppression does not lie outside the mind. These are all just manifestations of intentions, outcroppings of thoughts driven by greed, by hatred, by delusion.

But when the intentions are right, the actions will be right, and for the intentions to be right the surest guarantee is right views. One who recognizes the law of *kamma,* that actions bring retributive consequences, will frame his pursuits to accord with this law; thus his actions, expressive of his intentions, will conform to the canons of right conduct. The Buddha succinctly sums up the matter when he says that for a person who holds a wrong view, his deeds, words, plans, and purposes grounded in that view will lead to suffering, while for a person who holds right view, his deeds, words, plans, and purposes grounded in that view will lead to happiness.[3]

Since the most important formulation of right view is the understanding of the Four Noble Truths, it follows that this view should be in some way determinative of the content of right intention. This we find to be in fact the case. Understanding the four truths in relation to one's own life gives rise to the intention of renunciation; understanding them in relation to other beings gives rise to the other two right intentions. When we see how our own lives are pervaded by *dukkha*, and how this *dukkha* derives from craving, the mind inclines to renunciation—to abandoning craving and the objects to which it binds us. Then, when we apply the truths in an analogous way to other living beings, the contemplation nurtures the growth of good will and harmlessness. We see that, like ourselves, all other living beings want to be happy, and again that like ourselves they are subject to suffering. The consideration that all beings seek happiness causes thoughts of good will to arise—the loving wish that they be well, happy, and peaceful. The consideration that beings are exposed to suffering causes thoughts of harmlessness to arise—the compassionate wish that they be free from suffering.

The moment the cultivation of the Noble Eightfold Path begins, the factors of right view and right intention together start to counteract the three unwholesome roots. Delusion, the primary cognitive defilement, is opposed by right view, the nascent seed of wisdom. The complete eradication of delusion will only take place when right view is developed to the stage of full realization, but every flickering of correct understanding contributes to its eventual destruction. The other two roots, being emotive defilements, require opposition through the redirecting of intention, and thus meet their antidotes in thoughts of renunciation, good will, and harmlessness.

Since greed and aversion are deeply grounded, they do not yield easily; however, the work of overcoming them is not impossible if an effective strategy is employed. The path devised by the Buddha makes use of an indirect approach: it proceeds by tackling the thoughts to which these defilements give rise. Greed and aversion surface in the form of thoughts, and thus can be eroded by a process of "thought substitution," by replacing them with the thoughts opposed to them. The intention of renunciation provides the remedy to greed. Greed comes to manifestation in thoughts of desire—as sensual, acquisitive, and possessive thoughts. Thoughts of renunciation spring from the wholesome root of non-greed, which they activate whenever they are cultivated. Since contrary thoughts cannot coexist, when thoughts of renunciation are roused, they dislodge thoughts of desire, thus causing non-greed to replace greed. Similarly, the intentions of good will and harmlessness offer the antidote to aversion. Aversion comes to manifestation either in thoughts of ill will—as angry, hostile, or resentful thoughts; or in thoughts of harming—as the impulses to cruelty, aggression, and destruction. Thoughts of good will counter the former outflow of aversion, thoughts of harmlessness the latter outflow, in this way excising the unwholesome root of aversion itself.

The Intention of Renunciation

The Buddha describes his teaching as running contrary to the way of the world. The way of the world is the way of desire, and the unenlightened who follow this way flow with the current of desire, seeking happiness by pursuing the objects in which they imagine they will find fulfilment. The Buddha's message of renunciation states exactly the opposite: the pull of desire is to be resisted and eventually abandoned. Desire is to be abandoned not because it is morally evil but because it is a root of suffering.[4] Thus renunciation, turning away from craving and its drive for gratification, becomes the key to happiness, to freedom from the hold of attachment.

The Buddha does not demand that everyone leave the household life for the monastery or ask his followers to discard all sense enjoyments on the spot. The degree to which a person renounces depends on his or her disposition and situation. But what remains as a guiding principle is this: that the attainment of deliverance requires the complete eradication of craving, and progress along the path is accelerated to the extent that one overcomes craving. Breaking free from domination by desire may not be easy, but the difficulty does not abrogate the necessity. Since craving is the origin of *dukkha*, putting an end to *dukkha* depends on eliminating craving, and that involves directing the mind to renunciation.

But it is just at this point, when one tries to let go of attachment, that one encounters a powerful inner resistance. The mind does not want to relinquish its hold on the objects to which it has become attached. For such a long time it has been accustomed to gaining, grasping, and holding, that it seems impossible to break these habits by an act of will. One might agree to the need for renunciation, might want to leave attachment behind, but when the call is actually sounded the mind recoils and continues to move in the grip of its desires.

So the problem arises of how to break the shackles of desire. The Buddha does not offer as a solution the method of repression—the attempt to drive desire away with a mind full of fear and loathing. This approach does not resolve the problem but only pushes it below the surface, where it continues to thrive. The tool the Buddha holds out to free the mind from desire is understanding. Real renunciation is not a matter of compelling ourselves to give up things still inwardly cherished, but of changing our perspective on them so that they no longer bind us. When we understand the nature of desire, when we investigate it closely with keen attention, desire falls away by itself, without need for struggle.

To understand desire in such a way that we can loosen its hold, we need to see that desire is invariably bound up with *dukkha*. The whole phenomenon of desire, with its cycle of wanting and gratification, hangs on our way of seeing things. We remain in bondage to desire because we see it as our means to happiness. If we can look at desire from a different angle, its force will be abated, resulting in the move towards renunciation. What is needed to alter perception is something called "wise consideration" (*yoniso manasikāra*). Just as perception influences thought, so thought can influence perception. Our usual perceptions are tinged with "unwise consideration" (*ayoniso manasikāra*). We ordinarily look only at the surfaces of things, scan them in terms of our immediate interests and wants; only rarely do we dig into the roots of our involvements or explore their long-range consequences. To set this straight calls for wise consideration: looking into the hidden undertones to our actions, exploring their results, evaluating the worthiness of our goals. In this investigation our concern must not be with what is pleasant but with what is true. We have to be prepared and willing to discover what is true even at the cost of our comfort. For real security always lies on the side of truth, not on the side of comfort.

When desire is scrutinized closely, we find that it is constantly shadowed by *dukkha*. Sometimes *dukkha* appears as pain or irritation; often it lies low as a constant strain of discontent. But the two—desire and *dukkha*—are inseparable concomitants. We can confirm this for ourselves by considering the whole cycle of desire. At the moment desire springs up it creates in us a sense of lack, the pain of want. To end this pain we struggle to fulfil the desire. If our effort fails, we experience frustration, disappointment, sometimes despair. But even the pleasure of success is not unqualified. We worry that we might lose the ground we have gained. We feel driven to secure our position, to safeguard our territory, to gain more, to rise higher, to establish tighter controls. The demands of desire seem endless, and each desire demands the eternal: it wants the things we get to last forever. But all the objects of desire are impermanent. Whether it be wealth, power, position, or other persons, separation is inevitable, and the pain that accompanies separation is proportional to the force of attachment: strong attachment brings much suffering; little attachment brings little suffering; no attachment brings no suffering.[5]

Contemplating the *dukkha* inherent in desire is one way to incline the mind to renunciation. Another way is to contemplate directly the benefits flowing from renunciation. To move from desire to renunciation is not, as might be imagined, to move from happiness to grief, from abundance to destitution. It is to pass from gross, entangling pleasures to an exalted happiness and peace, from a condition of servitude to one of self-mastery. Desire ultimately breeds fear and sorrow, but renunciation gives fearlessness and joy. It promotes the accomplishment of all three stages of the threefold training: it purifies conduct, aids concentration, and nourishes the seed of wisdom. The entire course of practice from start to finish can in fact be seen as an evolving process of renunciation culminating in Nibbāna as the ultimate stage of relinquishment, "the relinquishing of all foundations of existence" (*sabb'ūpadhipaṭinissagga*).

When we methodically contemplate the dangers of desire and the benefits of renunciation, gradually we steer our mind away from the domination of desire. Attachments are shed like the leaves of a tree, naturally and spontaneously. The changes do not come suddenly, but when there is persistent practice, there is no doubt that they will come. Through repeated contemplation one thought knocks away another, the intention of renunciation dislodges the intention of desire.

The Intention of Good Will

The intention of good will opposes the intention of ill will, thoughts governed by anger and aversion. As in the case of desire, there are two ineffective ways of handling ill will. One is to yield to it, to express the aversion by bodily or verbal action. This approach releases the tension, helps drive the anger "out of one's system," but it also poses certain dangers. It breeds resentment, provokes retaliation, creates enemies, poisons relationships, and generates unwholesome *kamma*; in the end, the ill will does not leave the "system" after all, but instead is driven down to a deeper level where it continues to vitiate one's thoughts and conduct. The other approach, repression, also fails to dispel the destructive force of ill will. It merely turns that force around and pushes it inward, where it becomes transmogrified into self-contempt, chronic depression, or a tendency to irrational outbursts of violence.

The remedy the Buddha recommends to counteract ill will, especially when the object is another person, is a quality called in Pāli *mettā*. This word derives from another word meaning "friend," but *mettā* signifies much more than ordinary friendliness. I prefer to translate it by the compound "lovingkindness," which best captures the intended sense: an intense feeling of selfless love for other beings radiating outwards as a heartfelt concern for their well-being and happiness. *Mettā* is not just sentimental good will, nor is it a conscientious response to a moral imperative or divine command. It must become a deep inner feeling, characterized by spontaneous warmth rather than by a sense of obligation. At its peak *mettā* rises to the heights of a *brahmavihāra*, a "divine dwelling," a total way of being centred on the radiant wish for the welfare of all living beings.

The kind of love implied by *mettā* should be distinguished from sensual love as well as from the love involved in personal affection. The first is a form of craving, necessarily self-directed, while the second still includes a degree of attachment: we love a person because that person gives us pleasure, belongs to our family or group, or reinforces our own self-image. Only rarely does the feeling of affection transcend all traces of ego-reference, and even then its scope is limited. It applies only to a certain person or group of people while excluding others.

The love involved in *mettā*, in contrast, does not hinge on particular relations to particular persons. Here the reference point of self is utterly omitted. We are concerned only with suffusing others with a mind of lovingkindness, which ideally is to be developed into a universal state, extended to all living beings without discriminations or reservations. The way to impart to *mettā* this universal scope is to cultivate it as an exercise in meditation. Spontaneous feelings of good will occur too sporadically and are too limited in range to be relied on as the remedy for aversion. The idea of deliberately developing love has been criticized as contrived, mechanical, and calculated. Love, it is said, can only be genuine when it is spontaneous, arisen without inner prompting or effort. But it is a Buddhist thesis that the mind cannot be commanded to love spontaneously; it can only be shown the means to develop love and enjoined to practise accordingly. At first the means has to be employed with some deliberation, but through practice the feeling of love becomes ingrained, grafted onto the mind as a natural and spontaneous tendency.

The method of development is *mettā-bhāvanā*, the meditation on lovingkindness, one of the most important kinds of Buddhist meditation. The meditation begins with the development of loving-kindness towards oneself.[6] It is suggested that one take oneself as the first object of *mettā* because true lovingkindness for others only becomes possible when one is able to feel genuine lovingkindness for oneself. Probably most of the anger and hostility we direct to others springs from negative attitudes we hold towards ourselves. When *mettā* is directed inwards towards oneself, it helps to melt down the hardened crust created by these negative attitudes, permitting a fluid diffusion of kindness and sympathy outwards.

Once one has learned to kindle the feeling of *mettā* towards oneself, the next step is to extend it to others. The extension of *mettā* hinges on a shift in the sense of identity, on expanding the sense of identity beyond its ordinary confines and learning to identify with others. The shift is purely psychological in method, entirely free from theological and metaphysical postulates, such as that of a universal self immanent in all beings. Instead, it proceeds from a simple, straightforward course of reflection which enables us to share the subjectivity of others and experience the world (at least imaginatively) from the standpoint of their own inwardness. The procedure starts with oneself. If we look into our own mind, we find that the basic urge of our being is the wish to be happy and free from suffering. Now, as soon as we see this in ourselves, we can immediately understand that all living beings share the same basic wish. All want to be well, happy, and secure. To develop *mettā* towards others, what is to be done is to imaginatively share their own innate wish for happiness. We use our own desire for happiness as the key, experience this desire as the basic urge of others, then come back to our own position and extend to them the wish that they may achieve their ultimate objective, that they may be well and happy.

The methodical radiation of *mettā* is practised first by directing *mettā* to individuals representing certain groups. These groups are set in an order of progressive remoteness from oneself. The radiation begins with a dear person, such as a parent or teacher, then moves on to a friend, then to a neutral person, then finally to a hostile person. Though the types are defined by their relation to oneself, the love to be developed is not based on that relation but on each person's common aspiration for happiness. With each individual one has to bring his (or her) image into focus and radiate the thought: "May he (she) be well! May he (she) be happy! May he (she) be peaceful!"[7] Only when one succeeds in generating a warm feeling of good will and kindness towards that person should one turn to the next. Once one gains some success with individuals, one can then work with larger units. One can try developing *mettā* towards all friends, all neutral persons, all hostile persons. Then *mettā* can be widened by directional suffusion, proceeding in the various directions—east, south, west, north, above, below—then it can be extended to all beings without distinction. In the end one suffuses the entire world with a mind of lovingkindness "vast, sublime, and immeasurable, without enmity, without aversion."

The Intention of Harmlessness

The intention of harmlessness is thought guided by compassion (*karuṇā*), aroused in opposition to cruel, aggressive, and violent thoughts. Compassion supplies the complement to lovingkindness. Whereas lovingkindness has the characteristic of wishing for the happiness and welfare of others, compassion has the characteristic of wishing that others be free from suffering, a wish to be extended without limits to all living beings. Like *mettā*, compassion arises by entering into the subjectivity of others, by sharing their interiority in a deep and total way. It springs up by considering that all beings, like ourselves, wish to be free from suffering, yet despite their wishes continue to be harassed by pain, fear, sorrow, and other forms of *dukkha*.

To develop compassion as a meditative exercise, it is most effective to start with somebody who is actually undergoing suffering, since this provides the natural object for compassion. One contemplates this person's suffering, either directly or imaginatively, then reflects that like oneself, he (she) also wants to be free from suffering. The thought should be repeated, and contemplation continually exercised, until a strong feeling of compassion swells up in the heart. Then, using that feeling as a standard, one turns to different individuals, considers how they are each exposed to suffering, and radiates the gentle feeling of compassion out to them. To increase the breadth and intensity of compassion it is helpful to contemplate the various sufferings to which living beings are susceptible. A useful guideline to this extension is provided by the first noble truth, with its enumeration of the different aspects of *dukkha*. One contemplates beings as subject to old age, then as subject to sickness, then to death, then to sorrow, lamentation, pain, grief, and despair, and so forth.

When a high level of success has been achieved in generating compassion by the contemplation of beings who are directly afflicted by suffering, one can then move on to consider people who are presently enjoying happiness which they have acquired by immoral means. One might reflect that such people, despite their superficial fortune, are doubtlessly troubled deep within by the pangs of conscience. Even if they display no outward signs of inner distress, one knows that they will eventually reap the bitter fruits of their evil deeds, which will bring them intense suffering. Finally, one can widen the scope of one's contemplation to include all living beings. One should contemplate all beings as subject to the universal suffering of *saṃsāra*, driven by their greed, aversion, and delusion through the round of repeated birth and death. If compassion is initially difficult to arouse towards beings who are total strangers, one can strengthen it by reflecting on the Buddha's dictum that in this beginningless cycle of rebirths, it is hard to find even a single being who has not at some time been one's own mother or father, sister or brother, son or daughter.

To sum up, we see that the three kinds of right intention—of renunciation, good will, and harmlessness—counteract the three wrong intentions of desire, ill will, and harmfulness. The importance of putting into practice the contemplations leading to the arising of these thoughts cannot be overemphasized. The contemplations have been taught as methods for cultivation, not mere theoretical excursions. To develop the intention of renunciation we have to contemplate the suffering tied up with the quest for worldly enjoyment; to develop the intention of good will we have to consider how all beings desire happiness; to develop the intention of harmlessness we have to consider how all beings wish to be free from suffering. The unwholesome thought is like a rotten peg lodged in the mind; the wholesome thought is like a new peg suitable to replace it. The actual contemplation functions as the hammer used to drive out the old peg with the new one. The work of driving in the new peg is practice—practising again and again, as often as is necessary to reach success. The Buddha gives us his assurance that the victory can be achieved. He says that whatever one reflects upon frequently becomes the inclination of the mind. If one frequently thinks sensual, hostile, or harmful thoughts, desire, ill will, and harmfulness become the inclination of the mind. If one frequently thinks in the opposite way, renunciation, good will, and harmlessness become the inclination of the mind (MN 19). The direction we take always comes back to ourselves, to the intentions we generate moment by moment in the course of our lives.

IV

Right Speech, Right Action, Right Livelihood
(Sammā Vācā, Sammā Kammanta, Sammā Ājīva)

The next three path factors—right speech, right action, and right livelihood—may be treated together, as collectively they make up the first of the three divisions of the path, the division of moral discipline (*sīlakkhandha*). Though the principles laid down in this section restrain immoral actions and promote good conduct, their ultimate purpose is not so much ethical as spiritual. They are not prescribed merely as guides to action, but primarily as aids to mental purification. As a necessary measure for human well-being, ethics has its own justification in the Buddha's teaching and its importance cannot be underrated. But in the special context of the Noble Eightfold Path ethical principles are subordinate to the path's governing goal, final deliverance from suffering. Thus for the moral training to become a proper part of the path, it has to be taken up under the tutelage of the first two factors, right view and right intention, and to lead beyond to the trainings in concentration and wisdom.

Though the training in moral discipline is listed first among the three groups of practices, it should not be regarded lightly. It is the foundation for the entire path, essential for the success of the other trainings. The Buddha himself frequently urged his disciples to adhere to the rules of discipline, "seeing danger in the slightest fault." One time, when a monk approached the Buddha and asked for the training in brief, the Buddha told him: "First establish yourself in the starting point of wholesome states, that is, in purified moral discipline and in right view. Then, when your moral discipline is purified and your view straight, you should practise the four foundations of mindfulness" (SN 47:3).

The Pāli word we have been translating as "moral discipline," *sīla*, appears in the texts with several overlapping meanings all connected with right conduct. In some contexts it means action conforming to moral principles, in others the principles themselves, in still others the virtuous qualities of character that result from the observance of moral principles. *Sīla* in the sense of precepts or principles represents the formalistic side of the ethical training, *sīla* as virtue the animating spirit, and *sīla* as right conduct the expression of virtue in real-life situations. Often *sīla* is formally defined as abstinence from unwholesome bodily and verbal action. This definition, with its stress on outer action, appears superficial. Other explanations, however, make up for the deficiency and reveal that there is more to *sīla* than is evident at first glance. The Abhidhamma, for example, equates *sīla* with the mental factors of abstinence (*viratiyo*)—right speech, right action, and right livelihood—an equation which makes it clear that what is really being cultivated through the observance of moral precepts is the mind. Thus while the training in *sīla* brings the "public" benefit of inhibiting socially detrimental actions, it entails the personal benefit of mental purification, preventing the defilements from dictating to us what lines of conduct we should follow.

The English word "morality" and its derivatives suggest a sense of obligation and constraint quite foreign to the Buddhist conception of *sīla*; this connotation probably enters from the theistic background to Western ethics. Buddhism, with its non-theistic framework, grounds its ethics, not on the notion of obedience, but on that of harmony. In fact, the commentaries explain the word *sīla* by another word, *samādhāna,* meaning "harmony" or "coordination."

The observance of *sīla* leads to harmony at several levels—social, psychological, kammic, and contemplative. At the social level the principles of *sīla* help to establish harmonious interpersonal relations, welding the mass of differently constituted members of society with their own private interests and goals into a cohesive social order in which conflict, if not utterly eliminated, is at least reduced. At the psychological level *sīla* brings harmony to the mind, protection from the inner split caused by guilt and remorse over moral transgressions. At the kammic level the observance of *sīla* ensures harmony with the cosmic law of *kamma,* hence favourable results in the course of future movement through the round of repeated birth and death. And at the fourth level, the contemplative, *sīla* helps establish the preliminary purification of mind to be completed, in a deeper and more thorough way, by the methodical development of serenity and insight.

When briefly defined, the factors of moral training are usually worded negatively, in terms of abstinence. But there is more to *sīla* than refraining from what is wrong. Each principle embedded in the precepts, as we will see, actually has two aspects, both essential to the training as a whole. One is abstinence from the unwholesome, the other commitment to the wholesome; the former is called "avoidance" (*vāritta*) and the latter "performance" (*cāritta*). At the outset of training the Buddha stresses the aspect of avoidance. He does so, not because abstinence from the unwholesome is sufficient in itself, but to establish the steps of practice in proper sequence. The steps are set out in their natural order (more logical than temporal) in the famous dictum of the Dhammapada: "To abstain from all evil, to cultivate the good, and to purify one's mind—this is the teaching of the Buddhas" (v. 183). The other two steps—cultivating the good and purifying the mind—also receive their due, but to ensure their success, a resolve to avoid the unwholesome is a necessity. Without such a resolve the attempt to develop wholesome qualities is bound to issue in a warped and stunted pattern of growth.

The training in moral discipline governs the two principal channels of outer action, speech and body, as well as another area of vital concern—one's way of earning a living. Thus the training contains three factors: right speech, right action, and right livelihood. These we will now examine individually, following the order in which they are set forth in the usual exposition of the path.

Right Speech (*sammā vācā*)

The Buddha divides right speech into four components: abstaining from false speech, abstaining from slanderous speech, abstaining from harsh speech, and abstaining from idle chatter. Because the effects of speech are not as immediately evident as those of bodily action, its importance and potential is easily overlooked. But a little reflection will show that speech and its offshoot, the written word, can have enormous consequences for good or for harm. In fact, whereas for beings such as animals who live at the preverbal level physical action is of dominant concern, for humans immersed in verbal communication speech gains the ascendency. Speech can break lives, create enemies, and start wars, or it can give wisdom, heal divisions, and create peace. This has always been so, yet in the modern age the positive and negative potentials of speech have been vastly multiplied by the tremendous increase in the means, speed, and range of communications. The capacity for verbal expression, oral and written, has often been regarded as the distinguishing mark of the human species. From this we can appreciate the need to make this capacity the means to human excellence rather than, as too often has been the case, the sign of human degradation.

(1) *Abstaining from false speech*
    (*musāvādā veramaṇī*)

> Herein someone avoids false speech and abstains from it. He speaks the truth, is devoted to truth, reliable, worthy of confidence, not a deceiver of people. Being at a meeting, or amongst people, or in the midst of his relatives, or in a society, or in the king's court, and called upon and asked as witness to tell what he knows, he answers, if he knows nothing: "I know nothing," and if he knows, he answers: "I know"; if he has seen nothing, he answers: "I have seen nothing," and if he has seen, he answers: "I have seen." Thus he never knowingly speaks a lie, either for the sake of his own advantage, or for the sake of another person's advantage, or for the sake of any advantage whatsoever.[1]

This statement of the Buddha discloses both the negative and the positive sides to the precept. The negative side is abstaining from lying, the positive side speaking the truth. The determinative factor behind the transgression is the intention to deceive. If one speaks something false believing it to be true, there is no breach of the precept as the intention to deceive is absent. Though the deceptive intention is common to all cases of false speech, lies can appear in different guises depending on the motivating root, whether greed, hatred, or delusion. Greed as the chief motive results in the lie aimed at gaining some personal advantage for oneself or for those close to oneself—material wealth, position, respect, or admiration. With hatred as the motive, false speech takes the form of the malicious lie, the lie intended to hurt and damage others. When delusion is the principal motive, the result is a less pernicious type of falsehood: the irrational lie, the compulsive lie, the interesting exaggeration, lying for the sake of a joke.

The Buddha's stricture against lying rests upon several reasons. For one thing, lying is disruptive to social cohesion. People can live together in society only in an atmosphere of mutual trust, where they have reason to believe that others will speak the truth; by destroying the grounds for trust and inducing mass suspicion, widespread lying becomes the harbinger signalling the fall from social solidarity to chaos. But lying has other consequences of a deeply personal nature at least equally disastrous. By their very nature lies tend to proliferate. Lying once and finding our word suspect, we feel compelled to lie again to defend our credibility, to paint a consistent picture of events. So the process repeats itself: the lies stretch, multiply, and connect until they lock us into a cage of falsehoods from which it is difficult to escape. The lie is thus a miniature paradigm for the whole process of subjective illusion. In each case the self-assured creator, sucked in by his own deceptions, eventually winds up their victim.

Such considerations probably lie behind the words of counsel the Buddha spoke to his son, the young novice Rāhula, soon after the boy was ordained. One day the Buddha came to Rāhula, pointed to a bowl with a little bit of water in it, and asked: "Rāhula, do you see this bit of water left in the bowl?" Rāhula answered: "Yes, sir." "So little, Rāhula, is the spiritual achievement (*sāmañña*, lit. 'recluseship') of one who is not afraid to speak a deliberate lie." Then the Buddha threw the water away, put the bowl down, and said: "Do you see, Rāhula, how that water has been discarded? In the same way one who tells a deliberate lie discards whatever spiritual achievement he has made." Again he asked: "Do you see how this bowl is now empty? In the same way one who has no shame in speaking lies is empty of spiritual achievement." Then the Buddha turned the bowl upside down and said: "Do you see, Rāhula, how this bowl has been turned upside down? In the same way one who tells a deliberate lie turns his spiritual achievements upside down and becomes incapable of progress." Therefore, the Buddha concluded, one should not speak a deliberate lie even in jest.[2]

It is said that in the course of his long training for enlightenment over many lives, a bodhisatta can break all the moral precepts except the pledge to speak the truth. The reason for this is very profound, and reveals that the commitment to truth has a significance transcending the domain of ethics and even mental purification, taking us to the domains of knowledge and being. Truthful speech provides, in the sphere of interpersonal communication, a parallel to wisdom in the sphere of private understanding. The two are respectively the outward and inward modalities of the same commitment to what is real. Wisdom consists in the realization of truth, and truth (*sacca*) is not just a verbal proposition but the nature of things as they are. To realize truth our whole being has to be brought into accord with actuality, with things as they are, which requires that in communications with others we respect things as they are by speaking the truth. Truthful speech establishes a correspondence between our own inner being and the real nature of phenomena, allowing wisdom to rise up and fathom their real nature. Thus, much more than an ethical principle, devotion to truthful speech is a matter of taking our stand on reality rather than illusion, on the truth grasped by wisdom rather than the fantasies woven by desire.

(2) *Abstaining from slanderous speech*
(pisuṇāya vācāya veramaṇī)

> He avoids slanderous speech and abstains from it. What he has heard here he does not repeat there, so as to cause dissension there; and what he has heard there he does not repeat here, so as to cause dissension here. Thus he unites those that are divided; and those that are united he encourages. Concord gladdens him, he delights and rejoices in concord; and it is concord that he spreads by his words.[3]

Slanderous speech is speech intended to create enmity and division, to alienate one person or group from another. The motive behind such speech is generally aversion, resentment of a rival's success or virtues, the intention to tear down others by verbal denigrations. Other motives may enter the picture as well: the cruel intention of causing hurt to others, the evil desire to win affection for oneself, the perverse delight in seeing friends divided.

Slanderous speech is one of the most serious moral transgressions. The root of hate makes the unwholesome *kamma* already heavy enough, but since the action usually occurs after deliberation, the negative force becomes even stronger because premeditation adds to its gravity. When the slanderous statement is false, the two wrongs of falsehood and slander combine to produce an extremely powerful unwholesome *kamma.* The canonical texts record several cases in which the calumny of an innocent party led to an immediate rebirth in the plane of misery.

The opposite of slander, as the Buddha indicates, is speech that promotes friendship and harmony. Such speech originates from a mind of lovingkindness and sympathy. It wins the trust and affection of others, who feel they can confide in one without fear that their disclosures will be used against them. Beyond the obvious benefits that such speech brings in this present life, it is said that abstaining from slander has as its kammic result the gain of a retinue of friends who can never be turned against one by the slanderous words of others.[4]

(3) *Abstaining from harsh speech*
    (pharusāya vācāya veramaṇī)

> He avoids harsh language and abstains from it. He speaks such words as are gentle, soothing to the ear, loving, such words as go to the heart, and are courteous, friendly, and agreeable to many.[5]

Harsh speech is speech uttered in anger, intended to cause the hearer pain. Such speech can assume different forms, of which we might mention three. One is *abusive speech:* scolding, reviling, or reproving another angrily with bitter words. A second is *insult:* hurting another by ascribing to him some offensive quality which detracts from his dignity. A third is *sarcasm:* speaking to someone in a way which ostensibly lauds him, but with such a tone or twist of phrasing that the ironic intent becomes clear and causes pain.

The main root of harsh speech is aversion, assuming the form of anger. Since the defilement in this case tends to work impulsively, without deliberation, the transgression is less serious than slander and the kammic consequence generally less severe. Still, harsh speech is an unwholesome action with disagreeable results for oneself and others, both now and in the future, so it has to be restrained. The ideal antidote is patience—learning to tolerate blame and criticism from others, to sympathize with their shortcomings, to respect differences in viewpoint, to endure abuse without feeling compelled to retaliate. The Buddha calls for patience even under the most trying conditions:

> Even if, monks, robbers and murderers saw through your limbs and joints, whosoever should give way to anger thereat would not be following my advice. For thus ought you to train yourselves: "Undisturbed shall our mind remain, with heart full of love, and free from any hidden malice; and that person shall we penetrate with loving thoughts, wide, deep, boundless, freed from anger and hatred."[6]

(4) *Abstaining from idle chatter*
   (samphappalāpā veramaṇī)

> He avoids idle chatter and abstains from it. He speaks at the right time, in accordance with facts, speaks what is useful, speaks of the Dhamma and the discipline; his speech is like a treasure, uttered at the right moment, accompanied by reason, moderate and full of sense.[7]

Idle chatter is pointless talk, speech that lacks purpose or depth. Such speech communicates nothing of value, but only stirs up the defilements in one's own mind and in others. The Buddha advises that idle talk should be curbed and speech restricted as much as possible to matters of genuine importance. In the case of a monk, the typical subject of the passage just quoted, his words should be selective and concerned primarily with the Dhamma. Lay persons will have more need for affectionate small talk with friends and family, polite conversation with acquaintances, and talk in connection with their line of work. But even then they should be mindful not to let the conversation stray into pastures where the restless mind, always eager for something sweet or spicy to feed on, might find the chance to indulge its defiling propensities.

The traditional exegesis of abstaining from idle chatter refers only to avoiding engagement in such talk oneself. But today it might be of value to give this factor a different slant, made imperative by certain developments peculiar to our own time, unknown in the days of the Buddha and the ancient commentators. This is avoiding exposure to the idle chatter constantly bombarding us through the new media of communication created by modern technology. An incredible array of devices—television, radio, newspapers, pulp journals, the cinema—turns out a continuous stream of needless information and distracting entertainment the net effect of which is to leave the mind passive, vacant, and sterile. All these developments, naively accepted as "progress," threaten to blunt our aesthetic and spiritual sensitivities and deafen us to the higher call of the contemplative life. Serious aspirants on the path to liberation have to be extremely discerning in what they allow themselves to be exposed to. They would greatly serve their aspirations by including these sources of amusement and needless information in the category of idle chatter and making an effort to avoid them.

Right Action (*sammā kammanta*)

Right action means refraining from unwholesome deeds that occur with the body as their natural means of expression. The pivotal element in this path factor is the mental factor of abstinence, but because this abstinence applies to actions performed through the body, it is called "right action." The Buddha mentions three components of right action: abstaining from taking life, abstaining from taking what is not given, and abstaining from sexual misconduct. These we will briefly discuss in order.

(1) *Abstaining from the taking of life*
   (*pāṇātipātā veramaṇī*)

   Herein someone avoids the taking of life and abstains from it. Without stick or sword, conscientious, full of sympathy, he is desirous of the welfare of all sentient beings.[8]

"Abstaining from taking life" has a wider application than simply refraining from killing other human beings. The precept enjoins abstaining from killing any sentient being. A "sentient being" (pāṇī, satta) is a living being endowed with mind or consciousness; for practical purposes, this means human beings, animals, and insects. Plants are not considered to be sentient beings; though they exhibit some degree of sensitivity, they lack full-fledged consciousness, the defining attribute of a sentient being.

The "taking of life" that is to be avoided is intentional killing, the deliberate destruction of life of a being endowed with consciousness. The principle is grounded in the consideration that all beings love life and fear death, that all seek happiness and are averse to pain. The essential determinant of transgression is the volition to kill, issuing in an action that deprives a being of life. Suicide is also generally regarded as a violation, but not accidental killing as the intention to destroy life is absent. The abstinence may be taken to apply to two kinds of action, the primary and the secondary. The primary is the actual destruction of life; the secondary is deliberately harming or torturing another being without killing it.

While the Buddha's statement on non-injury is quite simple and straightforward, later commentaries give a detailed analysis of the principle. A treatise from Thailand, written by an erudite Thai patriarch, collates a mass of earlier material into an especially thorough treatment, which we shall briefly summarize here.[9] The treatise points out that the taking of life may have varying degrees of moral weight entailing different consequences. The three primary variables governing moral weight are the object, the motive, and the effort. With regard to the object there is a difference in seriousness between killing a human being and killing an animal, the former being kammically heavier since man has a more highly developed moral sense and greater spiritual potential than animals. Among human beings, the degree of kammic weight depends on the qualities of the person killed and his relation to the killer; thus killing a person of superior spiritual qualities or a personal benefactor, such as a parent or a teacher, is an especially grave act.

The motive for killing also influences moral weight. Acts of killing can be driven by greed, hatred, or delusion. Of the three, killing motivated by hatred is the most serious, and the weight increases to the degree that the killing is premeditated. The force of effort involved also contributes, the unwholesome *kamma* being proportional to the force and the strength of the defilements.

The positive counterpart to abstaining from taking life, as the Buddha indicates, is the development of kindness and compassion for other beings. The disciple not only avoids destroying life; he dwells with a heart full of sympathy, desiring the welfare of all beings. The commitment to non-injury and concern for the welfare of others represent the practical application of the second path factor, right intention, in the form of good will and harmlessness.

(2) *Abstaining from taking what is not given*
   (*adinnādānā veramaṇī*)

   He avoids taking what is not given and abstains from it; what another person possesses of goods and chattel in the village or in the wood, that he does not take away with thievish intent.[10]

"Taking what is not given" means appropriating the rightful belongings of others with thievish intent. If one takes something that has no owner, such as unclaimed stones, wood, or even gems extracted from the earth, the act does not count as a violation even though these objects have not been given. But also implied as a transgression, though not expressly stated, is withholding from others what should rightfully be given to them.

Commentaries mention a number of ways in which "taking what is not given" can be committed. Some of the most common may be enumerated:

(1) *stealing:* taking the belongings of others secretly, as in house-breaking, pickpocketing, etc.;
(2) *robbery:* taking what belongs to others openly by force or threats;
(3) *snatching:* suddenly pulling away another's possession before he has time to resist;
(4) *fraudulence:* gaining possession of another's belongings by falsely claiming them as one's own;
(5) *deceitfulness:* using false weights and measures to cheat customers.[11]

The degree of moral weight that attaches to the action is determined by three factors: the value of the object taken; the qualities of the victim of the theft; and the subjective state of the thief. Regarding the first, moral weight is directly proportional to the value of the object. Regarding the second, the weight varies according to the moral qualities of the deprived individual. Regarding the third, acts of theft may be motivated either by greed or hatred. While greed is the most common cause, hatred may also be responsible as when one person deprives another of his belongings not so much because he wants them for himself as because he wants to harm the latter. Between the two, acts motivated by hatred are kammically heavier than acts motivated by sheer greed.

The positive counterpart to abstaining from stealing is honesty, which implies respect for the belongings of others and for their right to use their belongings as they wish. Another related virtue is contentment, being satisfied with what one has without being inclined to increase one's wealth by unscrupulous means. The most eminent opposite virtue is generosity, giving away one's own wealth and possessions in order to benefit others.

(3) *Abstaining from sexual misconduct*
   (*kāmesu micchā-cārā veramaṇī*)

   He avoids sexual misconduct and abstains from it. He has no intercourse with such persons as are still under the protection of father, mother, brother, sister or relatives, nor with married women, nor with female convicts, nor lastly, with betrothed girls.[12]

The guiding purposes of this precept, from the ethical standpoint, are to protect marital relations from outside disruption and to promote trust and fidelity within the marital union. From the spiritual standpoint it helps curb the expansive tendency of sexual desire and thus is a step in the direction of renunciation, which reaches its consummation in the observance of celibacy (*brahmacariya*) binding on monks and nuns. But for laypeople the precept enjoins abstaining from sexual relations with an illicit partner. The primary transgression is entering into full sexual union, but all other sexual involvements of a less complete kind may be considered secondary infringements.

The main question raised by the precept concerns who is to count as an illicit partner. The Buddha's statement defines the illicit partner from the perspective of the man, but later treatises elaborate the matter for both sexes.[13]

For a man, three kinds of women are considered illicit partners:

(1) A woman who is married to another man. This includes, besides a woman already married to a man, a woman who is not his legal wife but is generally recognized as his consort, who lives with him or is kept by him or is in some way acknowledged as his partner. All these women are illicit partners for men other than their own husbands. This class would also include a woman engaged to another man. But a widow or divorced woman is not out of bounds, provided she is not excluded for other reasons.

(2) A woman still under protection. This is a girl or woman who is under the protection of her mother, father, relatives, or others rightfully entitled to be her guardians. This provision rules out elopements or secret marriages contrary to the wishes of the protecting party.

(3) A woman prohibited by convention. This includes close female relatives forbidden as partners by social tradition, nuns and other women under a vow of celibacy, and those prohibited as partners by the law of the land.

From the standpoint of a woman, two kinds of men are considered illicit partners:

(1) For a married woman any man other than her husband is out of bounds. Thus a married woman violates the precept if she breaks her vow of fidelity to her husband. But a widow or divorcee is free to remarry.

(2) For any woman any man forbidden by convention, such as close relatives and those under a vow of celibacy, is an illicit partner.

Besides these, any case of forced, violent, or coercive sexual union constitutes a transgression. But in such a case the violation falls only on the offender, not on the one compelled to submit.

The positive virtue corresponding to the abstinence is, for lay-people, marital fidelity. Husband and wife should each be faithful and devoted to the other, content with the relationship, and should not risk a breakup to the union by seeking outside partners. The principle does not, however, confine sexual relations to the marital union. It is flexible enough to allow for variations depending on social convention. The essential purpose, as was said, is to prevent sexual relations which are hurtful to others. When mature independent people, though unmarried, enter into a sexual relationship through free consent, so long as no other person is intentionally harmed, no breach of the training factor is involved.

Ordained monks and nuns, including men and women who have undertaken the eight or ten precepts, are obliged to observe celibacy. They must abstain not only from sexual misconduct, but from all sexual involvements, at least during the period of their vows. The holy life at its highest aims at complete purity in thought, word, and deed, and this requires turning back the tide of sexual desire.

Right Livelihood (samma ajiva)
Right livelihood is concerned with ensuring that one earns one's living in a righteous way. For a lay disciple the Buddha teaches that wealth should be gained in accordance with certain standards. One should acquire it only by legal means, not illegally; one should acquire it peacefully, without coercion or violence; one should acquire it honestly, not by trickery or deceit; and one should acquire it in ways which do not entail harm and suffering for others.[14] The Buddha mentions five specific kinds of livelihood which bring harm to others and are therefore to be avoided: dealing in weapons, in living beings (including raising animals for slaughter as well as slave trade and prostitution), in meat production and butchery, in poisons, and in intoxicants (AN 5:177). He further names several dishonest means of gaining wealth which fall under wrong livelihood: practising deceit, treachery, soothsaying, trickery, and usury (MN 117). Obviously any occupation that requires violation of right speech and right action is a wrong form of livelihood, but other occupations, such as selling weapons or intoxicants, may not violate those factors and yet be wrong because of their consequences for others.

The Thai treatise discusses the positive aspects of right livelihood under the three convenient headings of rightness regarding actions, rightness regarding persons, and rightness regarding objects.[15] "Rightness regarding actions" means that workers should fulfil their duties diligently and conscientiously, not idling away time, claiming to have worked longer hours than they did, or pocketing the company's goods. "Rightness regarding persons" means that due respect and consideration should be shown to employers, employees, colleagues, and customers. An employer, for example, should assign his workers chores according to their ability, pay them adequately, promote them when they deserve a promotion and give them occasional vacations and bonuses. Colleagues should try to cooperate rather than compete, while merchants should be equitable in their dealings with customers. "Rightness regarding objects" means that in business transactions and sales the articles to be sold should be presented truthfully. There should be no deceptive advertising, misrepresentations of quality or quantity, or dishonest manoeuvers.

V

RIGHT EFFORT
(Sammā Vāyāma)

The purification of conduct established by the prior three factors serves as the basis for the next division of the path, the division of concentration (samādhikkhandha). This present phase of practice, which advances from moral restraint to direct mental training, comprises the three factors of right effort, right mindfulness, and right concentration. It gains its name from the goal to which it aspires, the power of sustained concentration, itself required as the support for insight-wisdom. Wisdom is the primary tool for deliverance, but the penetrating vision it yields can only open up when the mind has been composed and collected. Right concentration brings the requisite stillness to the mind by unifying it with undistracted focus on a suitable object. To do so, however, the factor of concentration needs the aid of effort and mindfulness. Right effort provides the energy demanded by the task, right mindfulness the steadying points for awareness.

The commentators illustrate the interdependence of the three factors within the concentration group with a simple simile. Three boys go to a park to play. While walking along they see a tree with flowering tops and decide they want to gather the flowers. But the flowers are beyond the reach even of the tallest boy. Then one friend bends down and offers his back. The tall boy climbs up, but still hesitates to reach for the flowers from fear of falling. So the third boy comes over and offers his shoulder for support. The first boy, standing on the back of the second boy, then leans on the shoulder of the third boy, reaches up, and gathers the flowers.[1]

In this simile the tall boy who picks the flowers represents concentration with its function of unifying the mind. But to unify the mind concentration needs support: the energy provided by right effort, which is like the boy who offers his back. It also requires the stabilizing awareness provided by mindfulness, which is like the boy who offers his shoulder. When right concentration receives this support, then empowered by right effort and balanced by right mindfulness it can draw in the scattered strands of thought and fix the mind firmly on its object.

Energy (*viriya*), the mental factor behind right effort, can appear in either wholesome or unwholesome forms. The same factor fuels desire, aggression, violence, and ambition on the one hand, and generosity, self-discipline, kindness, concentration, and understanding on the other. The exertion involved in right effort is a wholesome form of energy, but it is something more specific, namely, the energy in wholesome states of consciousness directed to liberation from suffering. This last qualifying phrase is especially important. For wholesome energy to become a contributor to the path it has to be guided by right view and right intention, and to work in association with the other path factors. Otherwise, as the energy in ordinary wholesome states of mind, it merely engenders an accumulation of merit that ripens within the round of birth and death; it does not issue in liberation from the round.

Time and again the Buddha has stressed the need for effort, for diligence, exertion, and unflagging perseverance. The reason why effort is so crucial is that each person has to work out his or her own deliverance. The Buddha does what he can by pointing out the path to liberation; the rest involves putting the path into practice, a task that demands energy. This energy is to be applied to the cultivation of the mind, which forms the focus of the entire path. The starting point is the defiled mind, afflicted and deluded; the goal is the liberated mind, purified and illuminated by wisdom. What comes in between is the unremitting effort to transform the defiled mind into the liberated mind. The work of self-cultivation is not easy—there is no one who can do it for us but ourselves—but it is not impossible. The Buddha himself and his accomplished disciples provide the living proof that the task is not beyond our reach. They assure us, too, that anyone who follows the path can accomplish the same goal. But what is needed is effort, the work of practice taken up with the determination: "I shall not give up my efforts until I have attained whatever is attainable by manly perseverance, energy, and endeavour."[2]

The nature of the mental process effects a division of right effort into four "great endeavours":

(1) to prevent the arising of unarisen unwholesome states;
(2) to abandon unwholesome states that have already arisen;
(3) to arouse wholesome states that have not yet arisen;
(4) to maintain and perfect wholesome states already arisen.

The unwholesome states (*akusalā dhammā*) are the defilements, and the thoughts, emotions, and intentions derived from them, whether breaking forth into action or remaining confined within. The wholesome states (*kusalā dhammā*) are states of mind untainted by defilements, especially those conducing to deliverance. Each of the two kinds of mental states imposes a double task. The unwholesome side requires that the defilements lying dormant be prevented from erupting and that the active defilements already present be expelled. The wholesome side requires that the undeveloped liberating factors first be brought into being, then persistently developed to the point of full maturity. Now we will examine each of these four divisions of right effort, giving special attention to their most fertile field of application, the cultivation of the mind through meditation.

(1) To prevent the arising of unarisen unwholesome states

Herein the disciple rouses his will to avoid the arising of evil, unwholesome states that have not yet arisen; and he makes effort, stirs up his energy, exerts his mind and strives.[3]

The first side of right effort aims at overcoming unwholesome states, states of mind tainted by defilements. Insofar as they impede concentration the defilements are usually presented in a fivefold set called the "five hindrances" (*pañcanīvaraṇā*): sensual desire, ill will, dullness and drowsiness, restlessness and worry, and doubt.[4] They receive the name "hindrances" because they block the path to liberation; they grow up and over the mind preventing calm and insight, the primary instruments for progress. The first two hindrances, sensual desire and ill will, are the strongest of the set, the most formidable barriers to meditative growth, representing, respectively, the unwholesome roots of greed and aversion. The other three hindrances, less toxic but still obstructive, are offshoots of delusion, usually in association with other defilements.

Sensual desire is interpreted in two ways. Sometimes it is understood in a narrow sense as lust for the "five strands of sense pleasure," i.e. agreeable sights, sounds, smells, tastes, and touches; sometimes a broader interpretation is given, by which the term becomes inclusive of craving in all its modes, whether for sense pleasures, wealth, power, position, fame, or anything else it can settle upon. The second hindrance, *ill will,* is a synonym for aversion. It comprises hatred, anger, resentment, repulsion of every shade, whether directed towards other people, towards oneself, towards objects, or towards situations. The third hindrance, *dullness and drowsiness,* is a compound of two factors linked together by their common feature of mental unwieldiness. One is dullness (*thīna*), manifest as mental inertia; the other is drowsiness (*middha*), seen in mental sinking, heaviness of mind, or excessive inclination to sleep. At the opposite extreme is the fourth hindrance, *restlessness and worry.* This too is a compound with its two members linked by their common feature of disquietude. Restlessness (*uddhacca*) is agitation or excitement, which drives the mind from thought to thought with speed and frenzy; worry (*kukkucca*) is remorse over past mistakes and anxiety about their possible undesired consequences. The fifth hindrance, *doubt,* signifies a chronic indecisiveness and lack of resolution: not the probing of critical intelligence, an attitude encouraged by the Buddha, but a persistent inability to commit oneself to the course of spiritual training due to lingering doubts concerning the Buddha, his doctrine, and his path.

The first effort to be made regarding the hindrances is the effort to prevent the unarisen hindrances from arising; this is also called the endeavour to restrain (*saṃvarappadhāna*). The effort to hold the hindrances in check is imperative both at the start of meditative training and throughout the course of its development. For when the hindrances arise, they disperse attention and darken the quality of awareness, to the detriment of calm and clarity. The hindrances do not come from outside the mind but from within. They appear through the activation of certain tendencies constantly lying dormant in the deep recesses of the mental continuum, awaiting the opportunity to surface.

Generally what sparks the hindrances into activity is the input afforded by sense experience. The physical organism is equipped with five sense faculties each receptive to its own specific kind of data—the eye to forms, the ear to sounds, the nose to smells, the tongue to tastes, the body to tangibles. Sense objects continuously impinge on the senses, which relay the information they receive to the mind, where it is processed, evaluated, and accorded an appropriate response. But the mind can deal with the impressions it receives in different ways, governed in the first place by the manner in which it attends to them. When the mind adverts to the incoming data carelessly, with unwise consideration (*ayoniso manasikāra*), the sense objects tend to stir up unwholesome states. They do this either directly, through their immediate impact, or else indirectly by depositing memory traces which later may swell up as the objects of defiled thoughts, images, and fantasies. As a general rule the defilement that is activated corresponds to the object: attractive objects provoke desire, disagreeable objects provoke ill will, and indeterminate objects provoke the defilements connected with delusion.

Since an uncontrolled response to the sensory input stimulates the latent defilements, what is evidently needed to prevent them from arising is control over the senses. Thus the Buddha teaches, as the discipline for keeping the hindrances in check, an exercise called the restraint of the sense faculties (*indriya-saṃvara*):

> When he perceives a form with the eye, a sound with the ear, an odour with the nose, a taste with the tongue, an impression with the body, or an object with the mind, he apprehends neither the sign nor the particulars. And he strives to ward off that through which evil and unwholesome states, greed and sorrow, would arise, if he remained with unguarded senses; and he watches over his senses, restrains his senses.[5]

Restraint of the senses does not mean denial of the senses, retreating into a total withdrawal from the sensory world. This is impossible, and even if it could be achieved, the real problem would still not be solved; for the defilements lie in the mind, not in the sense organs or objects. The key to sense control is indicated by the phrase "not apprehending the sign or the particulars." The "sign" (*nimitta*) is the object's general appearance insofar as this appearance is grasped as the basis for defiled thoughts; the "particulars" (*anubyañjana*) are its less conspicuous features. If sense control is lacking, the mind roams recklessly over the sense fields. First it grasps the sign, which sets the defilements into motion, then it explores the particulars, which permits them to multiply and thrive.

To restrain the senses requires that mindfulness and clear understanding be applied to the encounter with the sense fields. Sense consciousness occurs in a series, as a sequence of momentary cognitive acts each having its own special task. The initial stages in the series occur as automatic functions: first the mind adverts to the object, then apprehends it, then admits the percept, examines it, and identifies it. Immediately following the identification a space opens up in which there occurs a free evaluation of the object leading to the choice of a response. When mindfulness is absent the latent defilements, pushing for an opportunity to emerge, will motivate a wrong consideration. One will grasp the sign of the object, explore its details, and thereby give the defilements their opportunity: on account of greed one will become fascinated by an agreeable object, on account of aversion one will be repelled by a disagreeable object. But when one applies mindfulness to the sensory encounter, one nips the cognitive process in the bud before it can evolve into the stages that stimulate the dormant taints. Mindfulness holds the hindrances in check by keeping the mind at the level of what is sensed. It rivets awareness on the given, preventing the mind from embellishing the datum with ideas born of greed, aversion, and delusion. Then, with this lucent awareness as a guide, the mind can proceed to comprehend the object as it is, without being led astray.

(2) To abandon the arisen unwholesome states

Herein the disciple rouses his will to overcome the evil, unwholesome states that have already arisen and he makes effort, stirs up his energy, exerts his mind and strives.[6]

Despite the effort at sense control the defilements may still surface. They swell up from the depths of the mental continuum, from the buried strata of past accumulations, to congeal into unwholesome thoughts and emotions. When this happens a new kind of effort becomes necessary, the effort to abandon arisen unwholesome states, called for short the endeavour to abandon (*pahānappadhāna*):

> He does not retain any thought of sensual lust, ill will, or harmfulness, or any other evil and unwholesome states that may have arisen; he abandons them, dispels them, destroys them, causes them to disappear.[7]

Just as a skilled physician has different medicines for different ailments, so the Buddha has different antidotes for the different hindrances, some equally applicable to all, some geared to a particular hindrance. In an important discourse the Buddha explains five techniques for expelling distracting thoughts.[8] The first is to expel the defiled thought with a wholesome thought which is its exact opposite, analogous to the way a carpenter might use a new peg to drive out an old one. For each of the five hindrances there is a specific remedy, a line of meditation designed expressly to deflate it and destroy it. This remedy can be applied intermittently, when a hindrance springs up and disrupts meditation on the primary subject; or it can be taken as a primary subject itself, used to counter a defilement repeatedly seen to be a persistent obstacle to one's practice. But for the antidote to become effective in the first role, as a temporary expedient required by the upsurge of a hindrance, it is best to gain some familiarity with it by making it a primary object, at least for short periods.

For desire a remedy of general application is the meditation on impermanence, which knocks away the underlying prop of clinging, the implicit assumption that the objects clung to are stable and durable. For desire in the specific form of sensual lust the most potent antidote is the contemplation of the unattractive nature of the body, to be dealt with at greater length in the next chapter. Ill will meets its proper remedy in the meditation on lovingkindness (*mettā*), which banishes all traces of hatred and anger through the methodical radiation of the altruistic wish that all beings be well and happy. The dispelling of dullness and drowsiness calls for a special effort to arouse energy, for which several methods are suggested: the visualization of a brilliant ball of light, getting up and doing a period of brisk walking meditation, reflection on death, or simply making a firm determination to continue striving. Restlessness and worry are most effectively countered by turning the mind to a simple object that tends to calm it down; the method usually recommended is mindfulness of breathing, attention to the in-and-out flow of the breath. In the case of doubt the special remedy is investigation: to make inquiries, ask questions, and study the teachings until the obscure points become clear.[9]

Whereas this first of the five methods for expelling the hindrances involves a one-to-one alignment between a hindrance and its remedy, the other four utilize general approaches. The second marshals the forces of shame (*hiri*) and moral dread (*ottappa*) to abandon the unwanted thought: one reflects on the thought as vile and ignoble or considers its undesirable consequences until an inner revulsion sets in which drives the thought away. The third method involves a deliberate diversion of attention. When an unwholesome thought arises and clamours to be noticed, instead of indulging it one simply shuts it out by redirecting one's attention elsewhere, as if closing one's eyes or looking away to avoid an unpleasant sight. The fourth method uses the opposite approach. Instead of turning away from the unwanted thought, one confronts it directly as an object, scrutinizes its features, and investigates its source. When this is done the thought quiets down and eventually disappears. For an unwholesome thought is like a thief: it only creates trouble when its operation is concealed, but put under observation it becomes tame. The fifth method, to be used only as a last resort, is suppression—vigorously restraining the unwholesome thought with the power of the will in the way a strong man might throw a weaker man to the ground and keep him pinned there with his weight.

By applying these five methods with skill and discretion, the Buddha says, one becomes a master of all the pathways of thought. One is no longer the subject of the mind but its master. Whatever thought one wants to think, that one will think. Whatever thought one does not want to think, that one will not think. Even if unwholesome thoughts occasionally arise, one can dispel them immediately, just as quickly as a red-hot pan will turn to steam a few chance drops of water.

(3) To arouse unarisen wholesome states

Herein the disciple rouses his will to arouse wholesome states that have not yet arisen; and he makes effort, stirs up his energy, exerts his mind and strives.[10]

Simultaneously with the removal of defilements, right effort also imposes the task of cultivating wholesome states of mind. This involves two divisions: the arousing of wholesome states not yet arisen and the maturation of wholesome states already arisen.

The first of the two divisions is also known as the endeavour to develop (*bhāvanāppadhāna*). Though the wholesome states to be developed can be grouped in various ways—serenity and insight, the four foundations of mindfulness, the eight factors of the path, etc.—the Buddha lays special stress on a set called the seven factors of enlightenment (*satta bojjhaṅgā*): mindfulness, investigation of phenomena, energy, rapture, tranquillity, concentration, and equanimity.

Thus he develops the factors of enlightenment, based on solitude, on detachment, on cessation, and ending in deliverance, namely: the enlightenment factors of mindfulness, investigation of phenomena, energy, rapture, tranquillity, concentration, and equanimity.[11]

The seven states are grouped together as "enlightenment factors" both because they lead to enlightenment and because they constitute enlightenment. In the preliminary stages of the path they prepare the way for the great realization; in the end they remain as its components. The experience of enlightenment, perfect and complete understanding, is just these seven components working in unison to break all shackles and bring final release from sorrow.

The way to enlightenment starts with *mindfulness*. Mindfulness clears the ground for insight into the nature of things by bringing to light phenomena in the now, the present moment, stripped of all subjective commentary, interpretations, and projections. Then, when mindfulness has brought the bare phenomena into focus, the factor of *investigation* steps in to search out their characteristics, conditions, and consequences. Whereas mindfulness is basically receptive, investigation is an active factor which unflinchingly probes, analyzes, and dissects phenomena to uncover their fundamental structures.

The work of investigation requires *energy,* the third factor of enlightenment, which mounts in three stages. The first, inceptive energy, shakes off lethargy and arouses initial enthusiasm. As the work of contemplation advances, energy gathers momentum and enters the second stage, perseverance, wherein it propels the practice without slackening. Finally, at the peak, energy reaches the third stage, invincibility, where it drives contemplation forward leaving the hindrances powerless to stop it.

As energy increases, the fourth factor of enlightenment is quickened. This is *rapture,* a pleasurable interest in the object. Rapture gradually builds up, ascending to ecstatic heights: waves of bliss run through the body, the mind glows with joy, fervour and confidence intensify. But these experiences, as encouraging as they are, still contain a flaw: they create an excitation verging on restlessness. With further practice, however, rapture subsides and a tone of quietness sets in signalling the rise of the fifth factor, *tranquillity.* Rapture remains present, but it is now subdued, and the work of contemplation proceeds with self-possessed serenity.

Tranquillity brings to ripeness *concentration,* the sixth factor, one-pointed unification of mind. Then, with the deepening of concentration, the last enlightenment factor comes into dominance. This is *equanimity,* inward poise and balance free from the two defects of excitement and inertia. When inertia prevails, energy must be aroused; when excitement prevails, it is necessary to exercise restraint. But when both defects have been vanquished the practice can unfold evenly without need for concern. The mind of equanimity is compared to the driver of a chariot when the horses are moving at a steady pace: he neither has to urge them forward nor to hold them back, but can just sit comfortably and watch the scenery go by. Equanimity has the same "on-looking" quality. When the other factors are balanced the mind remains poised watching the play of phenomena.

(4) To maintain arisen wholesome states

Herein the disciple rouses his will to maintain the wholesome things that have already arisen, and not to allow them to disappear, but to bring them to growth, to maturity, and to the full perfection of development; and he makes effort, stirs up his energy, exerts his mind and strives.[12]

This last of the four right efforts aims at maintaining the arisen wholesome factors and bringing them to maturity. Called the "endeavour to maintain" (*anurakkhaṇappadhāna*), it is explained as the effort to "keep firmly in the mind a favourable object of concentration that has arisen."[13] The work of guarding the object causes the seven enlightenment factors to gain stability and gradually increase in strength until they issue in the liberating realization. This marks the culmination of right effort, the goal in which the countless individual acts of exertion finally reach fulfilment.

VI

RIGHT MINDFULNESS
(Sammā Sati)

The Buddha says that the Dhamma, the ultimate truth of things, is directly visible, timeless, calling out to be approached and seen. He says further that it is always available to us, and that the place where it is to be realized is within oneself.[1] The ultimate truth, the Dhamma, is not something mysterious and remote, but the truth of our own experience. It can be reached only by understanding our experience, by penetrating it right through to its foundations. This truth, in order to become liberating truth, has to be known directly. It is not enough merely to accept it on faith, to believe it on the authority of books or a teacher, or to think it out through deductions and inferences. It has to be known by insight, grasped and absorbed by a kind of knowing which is also an immediate seeing.

What brings the field of experience into focus and makes it accessible to insight is a mental faculty called in Pāli *sati*, usually translated as "mindfulness." Mindfulness is presence of mind, attentiveness or awareness. Yet the kind of awareness involved in mindfulness differs profoundly from the kind of awareness at work in our usual mode of consciousness. All consciousness involves awareness in the sense of a knowing or experiencing of an object. But with the practice of mindfulness awareness is applied at a special pitch. The mind is deliberately kept at the level of *bare attention,* a detached observation of what is happening within us and around us in the present moment. In the practice of right mindfulness the mind is trained to remain in the present, open, quiet, and alert, contemplating the present event. All judgements and interpretations have to be suspended, or if they occur, just registered and dropped. The task is simply to note whatever comes up just as it is occurring, riding the changes of events in the way a surfer rides the waves on the sea. The whole process is a way of coming back into the present, of standing in the here and now without slipping away, without getting swept away by the tides of distracting thoughts.

It might be assumed that we are always aware of the present, but this is a mirage. Only seldom do we become aware of the present in the precise way required by the practice of mindfulness. In ordinary consciousness the mind begins a cognitive process with some impression given in the present, but it does not stay with it. Instead it uses the immediate impression as a springboard for building blocks of mental constructs which remove it from the sheer facticity of the datum. The cognitive process is generally interpretative. The mind perceives its object free from conceptualization only briefly. Then, immediately after grasping the initial impression, it launches on a course of ideation by which it seeks to interpret the object to itself, to make it intelligible in terms of its own categories and assumptions. To bring this about the mind posits concepts, joins the concepts into constructs—sets of mutually corroborative concepts—then weaves the constructs together into complex interpretative schemes. In the end the original direct experience has been overrun by ideation and the presented object appears only dimly through dense layers of ideas and views, like the moon through a layer of clouds.

The Buddha calls this process of mental construction *papañca,* "elaboration," "embellishment," or "conceptual proliferation." The elaborations block out the presentational immediacy of phenomena; they let us know the object only "at a distance," not as it really is. But the elaborations do not only screen cognition; they also serve as a basis for projections. The deluded mind, cloaked in ignorance, projects its own internal constructs outwardly, ascribing them to the object as if they really belonged to it. As a result, what we know as the final object of cognition, what we use as the basis for our values, plans, and actions, is a patchwork product, not the original article. To be sure, the product is not wholly illusion, not sheer fantasy. It takes what is given in immediate experience as its groundwork and raw material, but along with this it includes something else: the embellishments fabricated by the mind.

The springs for this process of fabrication, hidden from view, are the latent defilements. The defilements create the embellishments, project them outwardly, and use them as hooks for coming to the surface, where they cause further distortion. To correct the erroneous notions is the task of wisdom, but for wisdom to discharge its work effectively, it needs direct access to the object as it is in itself, uncluttered by the conceptual elaborations. The task of right mindfulness is to clear up the cognitive field. Mindfulness brings to light experience in its pure immediacy. It reveals the object as it is before it has been plastered over with conceptual paint, overlaid with interpretations. To practice mindfulness is thus a matter not so much of doing but of undoing: not thinking, not judging, not associating, not planning, not imagining, not wishing. All these "doings" of ours are modes of interference, ways the mind manipulates experience and tries to establish its dominance. Mindfulness undoes the knots and tangles of these "doings" by simply noting. It does nothing but note, watching each occasion of experience as it arises, stands, and passes away. In the watching there is no room for clinging, no compulsion to saddle things with our desires. There is only a sustained contemplation of experience in its bare immediacy, carefully and precisely and persistently.

Mindfulness exercises a powerful grounding function. It anchors the mind securely in the present, so it does not float away into the past and future with their memories, regrets, fears, and hopes. The mind without mindfulness is sometimes compared to a pumpkin, the mind established in mindfulness to a stone.[2] A pumpkin placed on the surface of a pond soon floats away and always remains on the water's surface. But a stone does not float away; it stays where it is put and at once sinks into the water until it reaches bottom. Similarly, when mindfulness is strong, the mind stays with its object and penetrates its characteristics deeply. It does not wander and merely skim the surface as the mind destitute of mindfulness does.

Mindfulness facilitates the achievement of both serenity and insight. It can lead to either deep concentration or wisdom, depending on the mode in which it is applied. Merely a slight shift in the mode of application can spell the difference between the course the contemplative process takes, whether it descends to deeper levels of inner calm culminating in the stages of absorption, the *jhānas,* or whether instead it strips away the veils of delusion to arrive at penetrating insight. To lead to the stages of serenity the primary chore of mindfulness is to keep the mind on the object, free from straying. Mindfulness serves as the guard charged with the responsibility of making sure that the mind does not slip away from the object to lose itself in random undirected thoughts. It also keeps watch over the factors stirring in the mind, catching the hindrances beneath their camouflages and expelling them before they can cause harm. To lead to insight and the realizations of wisdom, mindfulness is exercised in a more differentiated manner. Its task, in this phase of practice, is to observe, to note, to discern phenomena with utmost precision until their fundamental characteristics are brought to light.

Right mindfulness is cultivated through a practice called "the four foundations of mindfulness" (*cattāro satipaṭṭhānā*), the mindful contemplation of four objective spheres: the body, feelings, states of mind, and phenomena.[3] As the Buddha explains:

> And what, monks, is right mindfulness? Herein, a monk dwells contemplating the body in the body, ardent, clearly comprehending and mindful, having put away covetousness and grief concerning the world. He dwells contemplating feelings in feelings...states of mind in states of mind...phenomena in phenomena, ardent, clearly comprehending and mindful, having put away covetousness and grief concerning the world.[4]

The Buddha says that the four foundations of mindfulness form "the only way that leads to the attainment of purity, to the overcoming of sorrow and lamentation, to the end of pain and grief, to the entering upon the right path and the realization of Nibbāna."[5] They are called "the only way" (*ekāyano maggo*), not for the purpose of setting forth a narrow dogmatism, but to indicate that the attainment of liberation can only issue from the penetrating contemplation of the field of experience undertaken in the practice of right mindfulness.

Of the four applications of mindfulness, the contemplation of the body is concerned with the material side of existence; the other three are concerned principally (though not solely) with the mental side. The completion of the practice requires all four contemplations. Though no fixed order is laid down in which they are to be taken up, the body is generally taken first as the basic sphere of contemplation; the others come into view later, when mindfulness has gained in strength and clarity. Limitations of space do not allow for a complete explanation of all four foundations. Here we have to settle for a brief synopsis.

(1) Contemplation of the Body (*kāyānupassanā*)

The Buddha begins his exposition of the body with contemplation of the mindfulness of breathing (*ānāpānasati*). Though not required as a starting point for meditation, in actual practice mindfulness of breathing usually serves as the "root meditation subject" (*mūlakammaṭṭhāna*), the foundation for the entire course of contemplation. It would be a mistake, however, to consider this subject merely an exercise for neophytes. By itself mindfulness of breathing can lead to all the stages of the path culminating in full awakening. In fact it was this meditation subject that the Buddha used on the night of his own enlightenment. He also reverted to it throughout the years during his solitary retreats, and constantly recommended it to the monks, praising it as "peaceful and sublime, an unadulterated blissful abiding, which banishes at once and stills evil unwholesome thoughts as soon as they arise" (MN 118).

Mindfulness of breathing can function so effectively as a subject of meditation because it works with a process that is always available to us, the process of respiration. What it does to turn this process into a basis for meditation is simply to bring it into the range of awareness by making the breath an object of observation. The meditation requires no special intellectual sophistication, only awareness of the breath. One merely breathes naturally through the nostrils keeping the breath in mind at the contact point around the nostrils or upper lip, where the sensation of breath can be felt as the air moves in and out. There should be no attempt to control the breath or to force it into predetermined rhythms, only a mindful contemplation of the natural process of breathing in and out. The awareness of breath cuts through the complexities of discursive thinking, rescues us from pointless wandering in the labyrinth of vain imaginings, and grounds us solidly in the present. For whenever we become aware of breathing, really aware of it, we can be aware of it only in the present, never in the past or the future.

The Buddha's exposition of mindfulness of breathing involves four basic steps. The first two (which are not necessarily sequential) require that a long inhalation or exhalation be noted as it occurs, and that a short inhalation or exhalation be noted as it occurs. One simply observes the breath moving in and out, observing it as closely as possible, noting whether the breath is long or short. As mindfulness grows sharper, the breath can be followed through the entire course of its movement, from the beginning of an inhalation through its intermediary stages to its end, then from the beginning of an exhalation through its intermediary stages to its end. This third step is called "clearly perceiving the entire (breath) body." The fourth step, "calming the bodily function," involves a progressive quieting down of the breath and its associated bodily functions until they become extremely fine and subtle. Beyond these four basic steps lie more advanced practices which direct mindfulness of breathing towards deep concentration and insight.[6]

Another practice in the contemplation of the body, which extends meditation outwards from the confines of a single fixed position, is mindfulness of the postures. The body can assume four basic postures—walking, standing, sitting, and lying down—and a variety of other positions marking the change from one posture to another. Mindfulness of the postures focuses full attention on the body in whatever position it assumes: when walking one is aware of walking, when standing one is aware of standing, when sitting one is aware of sitting, when lying down one is aware of lying down, when changing postures one is aware of changing postures. The contemplation of the postures illuminates the impersonal nature of the body. It reveals that the body is not a self or the belonging of a self, but merely a configuration of living matter subject to the directing influence of volition.

The next exercise carries the extension of mindfulness a step further. This exercise, called "mindfulness and clear comprehension" (*satisampajañña*), adds to the bare awareness an element of understanding. When performing any action, one performs it with full awareness or clear comprehension. Going and coming, looking ahead and looking aside, bending and stretching, dressing, eating, drinking, urinating, defecating, falling asleep, waking up, speaking, remaining silent—all become occasions for the progress of meditation when done with clear comprehension. In the commentaries clear comprehension is explained as fourfold: (1) understanding the purpose of the action, i.e. recognizing its aim and determining whether that aim accords with the Dhamma; (2) understanding suitability, i.e. knowing the most efficient means to achieve one's aim; (3) understanding the range of meditation, i.e. keeping the mind constantly in a meditative frame even when engaged in action; and (4) understanding without delusion, i.e. seeing the action as an impersonal process devoid of a controlling ego-entity.[7] This last aspect will be explored more thoroughly in the last chapter, on the development of wisdom.

The next two sections on mindfulness of the body present analytical contemplations intended to expose the body's real nature. One of these is the meditation on the body's unattractiveness, already touched on in connection with right effort; the other, the analysis of the body into the four primary elements. The first, the meditation on unattractiveness,[8] is designed to counter infatuation with the body, especially in its form of sexual desire. The Buddha teaches that the sexual drive is a manifestation of craving, thus a cause of *dukkha* that has to be reduced and extricated as a precondition for bringing *dukkha* to an end. The meditation aims at weakening sexual desire by depriving the sexual urge of its cognitive underpinning, the perception of the body as sensually alluring. Sensual desire rises and falls together with this perception. It springs up because we view the body as attractive; it declines when this perception of beauty is removed. The perception of bodily attractiveness in turn lasts only so long as the body is looked at superficially, grasped in terms of selected impressions. To counter that perception we have to refuse to stop with these impressions but proceed to inspect the body at a deeper level, with a probing scrutiny grounded in dispassion.

Precisely this is what is undertaken in the meditation on unattractiveness, which turns back the tide of sensuality by pulling away its perceptual prop. The meditation takes one's own body as object, since for a neophyte to start off with the body of another, especially a member of the opposite sex, might fail to accomplish the desired result. Using visualization as an aid, one mentally dissects the body into its components and investigates them one by one, bringing their repulsive nature to light. The texts mention thirty-two parts: head-hairs, body-hairs, nails, teeth, skin, flesh, sinews, bones, marrow, kidneys, heart, liver, diaphragm, spleen, lungs, large intestines, small intestines, stomach contents, excrement, brain, bile, phlegm, pus, blood, sweat, fat, tears, grease, snot, spittle, sinovial fluid, and urine. The repulsiveness of the parts implies the same for the whole: the body seen closeup is truly unattractive, its beautiful appearance a mirage. But the aim of this meditation must not be misapprehended. The aim is not to produce aversion and disgust but detachment, to extinguish the fire of lust by removing its fuel.[9]

The other analytical contemplation deals with the body in a different way. This meditation, called the analysis into elements (*dhātuvavatthāna*), sets out to counter our innate tendency to identify with the body by exposing the body's essentially impersonal nature. The means it employs, as its name indicates, is the mental dissection of the body into the four primary elements, referred to by the archaic names earth, water, fire, and air, but actually signifying the four principal behavioural modes of matter: solidity, fluidity, heat, and oscillation. The solid element is seen most clearly in the body's solid parts—the organs, tissues, and bones; the fluid element, in the bodily fluids; the heat element, in the body's temperature; the oscillation element, in the respiratory process. The break with the identification of the body as "I" or "my self" is effected by a widening of perspective after the elements have come into view. Having analyzed the body into the elements, one then considers that all four elements, the chief aspects of bodily existence, are essentially identical with the chief aspects of external matter, with which the body is in constant interchange. When one vividly realizes this through prolonged meditation, one ceases to identify with the body, ceases to cling to it. One sees that the body is nothing more than a particular configuration of changing material processes which support a stream of changing mental processes. There is nothing here that can be considered a truly existent self, nothing that can provide a substantial basis for the sense of personal identity.[10]

The last exercise in mindfulness of the body is a series of

"cemetery meditations," contemplations of the body's disintegration after death, which may be performed either imaginatively, with the aid of pictures, or through direct confrontation with a corpse. By any of these means one obtains a clear mental image of a decomposing body, then applies the process to one's own body, considering: "This body, now so full of life, has the same nature and is subject to the same fate. It cannot escape death, cannot escape disintegration, but must eventually die and decompose." Again, the purpose of this meditation should not be misunderstood. The aim is not to indulge in a morbid fascination with death and corpses, but to sunder our egoistic clinging to existence with a contemplation sufficiently powerful to break its hold. The clinging to existence subsists through the implicit assumption of permanence. In the sight of a corpse we meet the teacher who proclaims unambiguously: "Everything formed is impermanent."

(2) Contemplation of Feeling (vedanānupassanā)

The next foundation of mindfulness is feeling (*vedanā*). The word "feeling" is used here, not in the sense of emotion (a complex phenomenon best subsumed under the third and fourth foundations of mindfulness), but in the narrower sense of the affective tone or "hedonic quality" of experience. This may be of three kinds, yielding three principal types of feeling: pleasant feeling, painful feeling, and neutral feeling. The Buddha teaches that feeling is an inseparable concomitant of consciousness, since every act of knowing is coloured by some affective tone. Thus feeling is present at every moment of experience; it may be strong or weak, clear or indistinct, but some feeling must accompany the cognition.

Feeling arises in dependence on a mental event called "contact" (*phassa*). Contact marks the "coming together" of consciousness with the object via a sense faculty; it is the factor by virtue of which consciousness "touches" the object presenting itself to the mind through the sense organ. Thus there are six kinds of contact distinguished by the six sense faculties—eye-contact, ear-contact, nose-contact, tongue-contact, body-contact, and mind-contact—and six kinds of feeling distinguished by the contact from which they spring.

Feeling acquires special importance as an object of contemplation because it is feeling that usually triggers the latent defilements into activity. The feelings may not be clearly registered, but in subtle ways they nourish and sustain the dispositions to unwholesome states. Thus when a pleasant feeling arises, we fall under the influence of the defilement greed and cling to it. When a painful feeling occurs, we respond with displeasure, hate, and fear, which are aspects of aversion. And when a neutral feeling occurs, we generally do not notice it, or let it lull us into a false sense of security—states of mind governed by delusion. From this it can be seen that each of the root defilements is conditioned by a particular kind of feeling: greed by pleasant feeling, aversion by painful feeling, delusion by neutral feeling.

But the link between feelings and the defilements is not a necessary one. Pleasure does not always have to lead to greed, pain to aversion, neutral feeling to delusion. The tie between them can be snapped, and one essential means for snapping it is mindfulness. Feeling will stir up a defilement only when it is not noticed, when it is indulged rather than observed. By turning it into an object of observation, mindfulness defuses the feeling so that it cannot provoke an unwholesome response. Then, instead of relating to the feeling by way of habit through attachment, repulsion, or apathy, we relate by way of contemplation, using the feeling as a springboard for understanding the nature of experience.

In the early stages the contemplation of feeling involves attending to the arisen feelings, noting their distinctive qualities: pleasant, painful, neutral. The feeling is noted without identifying with it, without taking it to be "I" or "mine" or something happening "to me." Awareness is kept at the level of bare attention: one watches each feeling that arises, seeing it as merely a feeling, a bare mental event shorn of all subjective references, all pointers to an ego. The task is simply to note the feeling's quality, its tone of pleasure, pain, or neutrality.

But as practice advances, as one goes on noting each feeling, letting it go and noting the next, the focus of attention shifts from the qualities of feelings to the process of feeling itself. The process reveals a ceaseless flux of feelings arising and dissolving, succeeding one another without a halt. Within the process there is nothing lasting. Feeling itself is only a stream of events, occasions of feeling flashing into being moment by moment, dissolving as soon as they arise. Thus begins the insight into impermanence, which, as it evolves, overturns the three unwholesome roots. There is no greed for pleasant feelings, no aversion for painful feelings, no delusion over neutral feelings. All are seen as merely fleeting and substance-less events devoid of any true enjoyment or basis for involvement.

(3) Contemplation of the State of Mind (*cittānupassanā*)

With this foundation of mindfulness we turn from a particular mental factor, feeling, to the general state of mind to which that factor belongs. To understand what is entailed by this contemplation it is helpful to look at the Buddhist conception of the mind. Usually we think of the mind as an enduring faculty remaining identical with itself through the succession of experiences. Though experience changes, the mind which undergoes the changing experience seems to remain the same, perhaps modified in certain ways but still retaining its identity. However, in the Buddha's teaching the notion of a permanent mental organ is rejected. The mind is regarded, not as a lasting subject of thought, feeling, and volition, but as a sequence of momentary mental acts, each distinct and discrete, their connections with one another causal rather than substantial.

A single act of consciousness is called a *citta,* which we shall render "a state of mind." Each *citta* consists of many components, the chief of which is consciousness itself, the basic experiencing of the object; consciousness is also called *citta,* the name for the whole being given to its principal part. Along with consciousness every *citta* contains a set of concomitants called *cetasikas,* mental factors. These include feeling, perception, volition, the emotions, etc.; in short, all the mental functions except the primary knowing of the object, which is *citta* or consciousness.

Since consciousness in itself is just a bare experiencing of an object, it cannot be differentiated through its own nature but only by way of its associated factors, the *cetasikas.* The *cetasikas* colour the *citta* and give it its distinctive character; thus when we want to pinpoint the *citta* as an object of contemplation, we have to do so by using the *cetasikas* as indicators. In his exposition of the contemplation of the state of mind, the Buddha mentions, by reference to *cetasikas,* sixteen kinds of *citta* to be noted: the mind with lust, the mind without lust, the mind with aversion, the mind without aversion, the mind with delusion, the mind without delusion, the cramped mind, the scattered mind, the developed mind, the undeveloped mind, the surpassable mind, the unsurpassable mind, the concentrated mind, the unconcentrated mind, the freed mind, the unfreed mind. For practical purposes it is sufficient at the start to focus solely on the first six states, noting whether the mind is associated with any of the unwholesome roots or free from them. When a particular *citta* is present, it is contemplated merely as a *citta*, a state of mind. It is not identified with as "I" or "mine," not taken as a self or as something belonging to a self. Whether it is a pure state of mind or a defiled state, a lofty state or a low one, there should be no elation or dejection, only a clear recognition of the state. The state is simply noted, then allowed to pass without clinging to the desired ones or resenting the undesired ones.

As contemplation deepens, the contents of the mind become increasingly rarefied. Irrelevant flights of thought, imagination, and emotion subside, mindfulness becomes clearer, the mind remains intently aware, watching its own process of becoming. At times there might appear to be a persisting observer behind the process, but with continued practice even this apparent observer disappears. The mind itself—the seemingly solid, stable mind—dissolves into a stream of cittas flashing in and out of being moment by moment, coming from nowhere and going nowhere, yet continuing in sequence without pause.

(4) Contemplation of Phenomena (*dhammānupassanā*)

In the context of the fourth foundation of mindfulness, the multivalent word *dhammā* (here intended in the plural) has two interconnected meanings, as the account in the sutta shows. One meaning is *cetasikas*, the mental factors, which are now attended to in their own right apart from their role as colouring the state of mind, as was done in the previous contemplation. The other meaning is the elements of actuality, the ultimate constituents of experience as structured in the Buddha's teaching.To convey both senses we render *dhammā* as "phenomena," for lack of a better alternative. But when we do so this should not be taken to imply the existence of some *noumenon* or substance behind

the phenomena.The point of the Buddha's teaching ᴏᴜ ᴀᴜ
egolessness, is that the basic constituents of actuality are bare
phenomena (*suddha-dhammā*) occurring without any noumenal
support.

The sutta section on the contemplation of phenomena is divided
into five sub-sections, each devoted to a different set of phenomena:
the five hindrances, the five aggregates, the six inner and outer
sense bases, the seven factors of enlightenment, and the Four Noble
Truths. Among these, the five hindrances and the seven enlightenment factors are *dhammā* in the narrower sense of mental factors,
the others are *dhammā* in the broader sense of constituents of
actuality. (In the third section, however, on the sense bases, there
is a reference to the fetters that arise through the senses; these can
also be included among the mental factors.) In the present chapter
we shall deal briefly only with the two groups that may be regarded
as *dhammā* in the sense of mental factors. We already touched on
both of these in relation to right effort (Chapter V); now we shall
consider them in specific connection with the practice of right
mindfulness. We shall discuss the other types of *dhammā*—the five
aggregates and the six senses—in the final chapter, in relation to
the development of wisdom.

The five hindrances and seven factors of enlightenment require
special attention because they are the principal impediments and
aids to liberation. The hindrances—sensual desire, ill will, dullness
and drowsiness, restlessness and worry, and doubt—generally
become manifest in an early stage of practice, soon after the
initial expectations and gross disturbances subside and the subtle
tendencies find the opportunity to surface. Whenever one of the
hindrances crops up, its presence should be noted; then, when it
fades away, a note should be made of its disappearance. To ensure
that the hindrances are kept under control an element of comprehension is needed: we have to understand how the hindrances
arise, how they can be removed, and how they can be prevented
from arising in the future.[11]

A similar mode of contemplation is to be applied to the seven factors of enlightenment: mindfulness, investigation, energy, rapture,
tranquillity, concentration, and equanimity. When any one of these
factors arises, its presence should be noted. Then, after noting its

presence, one has to investigate to discover how it arises and how it can be matured.[12] When they first spring up, the enlightenment factors are weak, but with consistent cultivation they accumulate strength. Mindfulness initiates the contemplative process. When it becomes well-established, it arouses investigation, the probing quality of intelligence. Investigation in turn calls forth energy, energy gives rise to rapture, rapture leads to tranquillity, tranquillity to one-pointed concentration, and concentration to equanimity. Thus the whole evolving course of practice leading to enlightenment begins with mindfulness, which remains throughout as the regulating power ensuring that the mind is clear, cognizant, and balanced.

VII

RIGHT CONCENTRATION
(Sammā Samādhi)

The eighth factor of the path is right concentration, in Pāli *sammā samādhi*. Concentration represents an intensification of a mental factor present in every state of consciousness. This factor, one-pointedness of mind (*citt'ekaggatā*), has the function of unifying the other mental factors in the task of cognition. It is the factor responsible for the individuating aspect of consciousness, ensuring that every *citta* or act of mind remains centred on its object. At any given moment the mind must be cognizant of something—a sight, a sound, a smell, a taste, a touch, or a mental object. The factor of one-pointedness unifies the mind and its other concomitants in the task of cognizing the object, while it simultaneously exercises the function of centring all the constituents of the cognitive act on the object. One-pointedness of mind explains the fact that in any act of consciousness there is a central point of focus, towards which the entire objective datum points from its outer peripheries to its inner nucleus.

However, *samādhi* is only a particular kind of one-pointedness; it is not equivalent to one-pointedness in its entirety. A gourmet sitting down to a meal, an assassin about to slay his victim, a soldier on the battlefield—these all act with a concentrated mind, but their concentration cannot be characterized as *samādhi*. *Samādhi* is exclusively wholesome one-pointedness, the concentration in a wholesome state of mind. Even then its range is still narrower: it does not signify every form of wholesome concentration, but only the intensified concentration that results from a deliberate attempt to raise the mind to a higher, more purified level of awareness.

The commentaries define *samādhi* as the centring of the mind and mental factors rightly and evenly on an object. *Samādhi*, as wholesome concentration, collects together the ordinarily dispersed and dissipated stream of mental states to induce an inner unification. The two salient features of a concentrated mind are unbroken attentiveness to an object and the consequent tranquillity of the mental functions, qualities which distinguish it from the unconcentrated mind. The mind untrained in concentration moves in a scattered manner which the Buddha compares to the flapping about of a fish taken from the water and thrown onto dry land. It cannot stay fixed but rushes from idea to idea, from thought to thought, without inner control. Such a distracted mind is also a deluded mind. Overwhelmed by worries and concerns, a constant prey to the defilements, it sees things only in fragments, distorted by the ripples of random thoughts. But the mind that has been trained in concentration, in contrast, can remain focused on its object without distraction. This freedom from distraction further induces a softness and serenity which make the mind an effective instrument for penetration. Like a lake unruffled by any breeze, the concentrated mind is a faithful reflector that mirrors whatever is placed before it exactly as it is.

The Development of Concentration
Concentration can be developed through either of two methods—either as the goal of a system of practice directed expressly towards the attainment of deep concentration at the level of absorption or as the incidental accompaniment of the path intended to generate insight. The former method is called the development of serenity (*samatha-bhāvanā*), the second the development of insight (*vipassanā-bhāvanā*). Both paths share certain preliminary requirements. For both, moral discipline must be purified, the various impediments must be severed, the meditator must seek out suitable instruction (preferably from a personal teacher), and must resort to a dwelling conducive to practice. Once these preliminaries have been dispensed with, the meditator on the path of serenity has to obtain an object of meditation, something to be used as a focal point for developing concentration.[1]

If the meditator has a qualified teacher, the teacher will probably assign him an object judged to be appropriate for his temperament. If he doesn't have a teacher, he will have to select an object himself, perhaps after some experimentation. The meditation manuals collect the subjects of serenity meditation into a set of forty, called "places of work" (*kammaṭṭhāna*) since they are the places where the meditator does the work of practice. The forty may be listed as follows:

ten *kasiṇas*

ten unattractive objects (*dasa asubhā*)

ten recollections (*dasa anussatiyo*)

four sublime states (*cattāro brahmavihārā*)

four immaterial states (*cattāro āruppā*)

one perception (*ekā saññā*)

one analysis (*eka vavatthāna*).

The *kasiṇas* are devices representing certain primordial qualities. Four represent the primary elements—the earth, water, fire, and air *kasiṇas*; four represent colours—the blue, yellow, red, and white *kasiṇas*; the other two are the light and the space *kasiṇas*. Each *kasiṇa* is a concrete object representative of the universal quality it signifies. Thus an earth *kasiṇa* would be a circular disk filled with clay. To develop concentration on the earth *kasiṇa* the meditator sets the disk in front of him, fixes his gaze on it, and contemplates "earth, earth." A similar method is used for the other *kasiṇas*, with appropriate changes to fit the case.

The ten "unattractive objects" are corpses in different stages of decomposition. This subject appears similar to the contemplation of bodily decay in the mindfulness of the body, and in fact in olden times the cremation ground was recommended as the most appropriate place for both. But the two meditations differ in emphasis. In the mindfulness exercise stress falls on the application of reflective thought, the sight of the decaying corpse serving as a stimulus for consideration of one's own eventual death and disintegration. In this exercise the use of reflective thought is discouraged. The stress instead falls on one-pointed mental fixation on the object, the less thought the better.

The ten recollections form a miscellaneous collection. The first three are devotional meditations on the qualities of the Triple Gem—the Buddha, the Dhamma, and the Sangha; they use as their basis standard formulas that have come down in the Suttas. The next three recollections also rely on ancient formulas: the meditations on morality, generosity, and the potential for divine-like qualities in oneself. Then come mindfulness of death, the contemplation of the unattractive nature of the body, mindfulness of breathing, and lastly, the recollection of peace, a discursive meditation on Nibbāna.

The four sublime states or "divine abodes" are the outwardly directed social attitudes—lovingkindness, compassion, sympathetic joy, and equanimity—developed into universal radiations which are gradually extended in range until they encompass all living beings. The four immaterial states are the objective bases for certain deep levels of absorption: the base of infinite space, the base of infinite consciousness, the base of nothingness, and the base of neither-perception-nor-non-perception. These become accessible as objects only to those who are already adept in concentration. The "one perception" is the perception of the repulsiveness of food, a discursive topic intended to reduce attachment to the pleasures of the palate. The "one analysis" is the contemplation of the body in terms of the four primary elements, already discussed in the chapter on right mindfulness.

When such a variety of meditation subjects is presented, the aspiring meditator without a teacher might be perplexed as to which to choose. The manuals divide the forty subjects according to their suitability for different personality types. Thus the unattractive objects and the contemplation of the parts of the body are judged to be most suitable for a lustful type, the meditation on lovingkindness to be best for a hating type, the meditation on the qualities of the Triple Gem to be most effective for a devotional type, etc. But for practical purposes the beginner in meditation can generally be advised to start with a simple subject that helps reduce discursive thinking. Mental distraction caused by restlessness and scattered thoughts is a common problem faced by persons of all different character types; thus a meditator of any temperament can benefit from a subject which promotes a slowing down and stilling of the thought process. The subject generally recommended for its effectiveness in clearing the mind of stray thoughts is mindfulness of breathing, which can therefore be suggested as the subject most suitable for beginners as well as veterans seeking a direct approach to deep concentration. Once the mind settles down and one's thought patterns become easier to notice, one might then make use of other subjects to deal with special problems that arise: the meditation on lovingkindness may be used to counteract anger and ill will, mindfulness of the bodily parts to weaken sensual lust, the recollection of the Buddha to inspire faith and devotion, the meditation on death to arouse a sense of urgency. The ability to select the subject appropriate to the situation requires skill, but this skill evolves through practice, often through simple trial-and-error experimentation.

The Stages of Concentration

Concentration is not attained all at once but develops in stages. To enable our exposition to cover all the stages of concentration, we will consider the case of a meditator who follows the entire path of serenity meditation from start to finish, and who will make much faster progress than the typical meditator is likely to make.

After receiving his meditation subject from a teacher, or selecting it on his own, the meditator retires to a quiet place. There he assumes the correct meditation posture—the legs crossed comfortably, the upper part of the body held straight and erect, hands placed one above the other on the lap, the head kept steady, the mouth and eyes closed (unless a *kasina* or other visual object is used), the breath flowing naturally and regularly through the nostrils. He then focuses his mind on the object and tries to keep it there, fixed and alert. If the mind strays, he notices this quickly, catches it, and brings it back gently but firmly to the object, doing this over and over as often as is necessary. This initial stage is called preliminary concentration (*parikkamma-samādhi*) and the object the preliminary sign (*parikkamma-nimitta*).

Once the initial excitement subsides and the mind begins to settle into the practice, the five hindrances are likely to arise, bubbling up from the depths. Sometimes they appear as thoughts, sometimes as images, sometimes as obsessive emotions: surges of desire, anger and resentment, heaviness of mind, agitation, doubts. The hindrances pose a formidable barrier, but with patience and sustained effort they can be overcome. To conquer them the meditator will have to be adroit. At times, when a particular hindrance becomes strong, he may have to lay aside his primary subject of meditation and take up another subject expressly opposed to the hindrance. At other times he will have to persist with his primary subject despite the bumps along the road, bringing his mind back to it again and again.

As he goes on striving along the path of concentration, his exertion activates five mental factors which come to his aid. These factors are intermittently present in ordinary undirected consciousness, but there they lack a unifying bond and thus do not play any special role. However, when activated by the work of meditation, these five factors pick up power, link up with one another, and steer the mind towards *samādhi*, which they will govern as the "*jhāna* factors," the factors of absorption (*jhānaṅga*). Stated in their usual order the five are: initial application of mind (*vitakka*), sustained application of mind (*vicāra*), rapture (*pīti*), happiness (*sukha*), and one-pointedness (*ekaggatā*).

Initial application of mind does the work of directing the mind to the object. It takes the mind, lifts it up, and drives it into the object the way one drives a nail through a block of wood. This done, *sustained application of mind* anchors the mind on the object, keeping it there through its function of examination. To clarify the difference between these two factors, initial application is compared to the striking of a bell, sustained application to the bell's reverberations. *Rapture*, the third factor, is the delight and joy that accompany a favourable interest in the object, while *happiness*, the fourth factor, is the pleasant feeling that accompanies successful concentration. Since rapture and happiness share similar qualities they tend to be confused with each other, but the two are not identical. The difference between them is illustrated by comparing rapture to the joy of a weary desert-farer who sees an oasis in the distance, happiness to his pleasure when drinking from the pond and resting in the shade. The fifth and final factor of absorption is *one-pointedness*, which has the pivotal function of unifying the mind on the object.[2]

When concentration is developed, these five factors spring up and counteract the five hindrances. Each absorption factor opposes a particular hindrance. Initial application of mind, through its work of lifting the mind up to the object, counters dullness and drowsiness. Sustained application, by anchoring the mind on the object, drives away doubt. Rapture shuts out ill will, happiness excludes restlessness and worry, and one-pointedness counters sensual desire, the most alluring inducement to distraction. Thus, with the strengthening of the absorption factors, the hindrances fade out and subside. They are not yet eradicated—eradication can only be effected by wisdom, the third division of the path—but they have been reduced to a state of quiescence where they cannot disrupt the forward movement of concentration.

At the same time that the hindrances are being overpowered by the *jhāna* factors inwardly, on the side of the object too, certain changes are taking place. The original object of concentration, the preliminary sign, is a gross physical object; in the case of a *kasiṇa*, it is a disk representing the chosen element or colour, in the case of mindfulness of breathing the touch sensation of the breath, etc. But with the strengthening of concentration the original object gives rise to another object called the "learning sign" (*uggaha-nimitta*). For a *kasiṇa* this will be a mental image of the disk seen as clearly in the mind as the original object was with the eyes; for the breath it will be a reflex image arisen from the touch sensation of the air currents moving around the nostrils.

When the learning sign appears, the meditator leaves off the preliminary sign and fixes his attention on the new object. In due time still another object will emerge out of the learning sign. This object, called the "counterpart sign" (*paṭibhāga-nimitta*), is a purified mental image many times brighter and clearer than the learning sign. The learning sign is compared to the moon seen behind a cloud, the counterpart sign to the moon freed from the cloud. Simultaneously with the appearance of the counterpart sign, the five absorption factors suppress the five hindrances, and the mind enters the stage of concentration called *upacāra-samādhi*, "access concentration." Here, in access concentration, the mind is drawing close to absorption. It has entered the "neighbourhood" (a possible meaning of *upacāra*) of absorption, but more work is still needed for it to become fully immersed in the object, the defining mark of absorption.

With further practice the factors of concentration gain in strength and bring the mind to absorption (*appanā-samādhi*). Like access concentration, absorption takes the counterpart sign as object. The two stages of concentration are differentiated neither by the absence of the hindrances nor by the counterpart sign as object;

these are common to both. What differentiates them is the strength of the *jhāna* factors. In access concentration the *jhāna* factors are present, but they lack strength and steadiness. Thus the mind in this stage is compared to a child who has just learned to walk: he takes a few steps, falls down, gets up, walks some more, and again falls down. But the mind in absorption is like a man who wants to walk: he just gets up and walks straight ahead without hesitation.

Concentration in the stage of absorption is divided into eight levels, each marked by greater depth, purity, and subtlety than its predecessor. The first four form a set called the four *jhānas*, a word best left untranslated for lack of a suitable equivalent, though it can be loosely rendered "meditative absorption."[3] The second four also form a set, the four immaterial states (*arūpā*). The eight have to be attained in progressive order, the achievement of any later level being dependent on the mastery of the immediately preceding level.

The four *jhānas* make up the usual textual definition of right concentration. Thus the Buddha says:

> And what, monks, is right concentration? Herein, secluded from sense pleasures, secluded from unwholesome states, a monk enters and dwells in the first *jhāna*, which is accompanied by initial and sustained application of mind and filled with rapture and happiness born of seclusion.
>
> Then, with the subsiding of initial and sustained application of mind, by gaining inner confidence and mental unification, he enters and dwells in the second *jhāna*, which is free from initial and sustained application but is filled with rapture and happiness born of concentration.
>
> With the fading out of rapture, he dwells in equanimity, mindful and clearly comprehending; and he experiences in his own person that bliss of which the noble ones say: "Happily lives he who is equanimous and mindful"—thus he enters and dwells in the third *jhāna*.
>
> With the abandoning of pleasure and pain and with the previous disappearance of joy and grief, he enters and dwells in the fourth *jhāna*, which has neither-pleasure-nor-pain and purity of mindfulness due to equanimity.
>
> This, monks, is right concentration.[4]

The *jhānas* are distinguished by way of their component factors. The first *jhāna* is constituted by the original set of five absorption factors: initial application, sustained application, rapture, happiness, and one-pointedness. After attaining the first *jhāna* the meditator is advised to master it. On the one hand he should not fall into complacency over his achievement and neglect sustained practice; on the other, he should not become over-confident and rush ahead to attain the next *jhāna*. To master the *jhāna* he should enter it repeatedly and perfect his skill in it, until he can attain it, remain in it, emerge from it, and review it without any trouble or difficulty.

After mastering the first *jhāna*, the meditator then considers that his attainment has certain defects. Though the *jhāna* is certainly far superior to ordinary sense consciousness, more peaceful and blissful, it still stands close to sense consciousness and is not far removed from the hindrances. Moreover, two of its factors, initial application and sustained application, appear in time to be rather coarse, not as refined as the other factors. Then the meditator renews his practice of concentration intent on overcoming initial and sustained application. When his faculties mature, these two factors subside and he enters the second *jhāna*. This *jhāna* contains only three component factors: rapture, happiness, and one-pointedness. It also contains a multiplicity of other constituents, the most prominent of which is confidence of mind.

In the second *jhāna* the mind becomes more tranquil and more thoroughly unified, but when mastered even this state seems gross, as it includes rapture, an exhilarating factor that inclines to excitation. So the meditator sets out again on his course of training, this time resolved on overcoming rapture. When rapture fades out, he enters the third *jhāna*. Here there are only two absorption factors, happiness and one-pointedness, while some other auxiliary states come into ascendency, most notably mindfulness, clear comprehension, and equanimity. But still, the meditator sees, this attainment is defective in that it contains the feeling of happiness, which is gross compared to neutral feeling, feeling that is neither pleasant not painful. Thus he strives to get beyond even the sublime happiness of the third *jhāna*. When he succeeds, he enters the fourth *jhāna*, which is defined by two factors—one-pointedness and neutral feeling—and has a special purity of mindfulness due to the high level of equanimity.

Beyond the four *jhānas* lie the four immaterial states, levels of absorption in which the mind transcends even the subtlest perception of visualized images still sometimes persisting in the *jhānas*. The immaterial states are attained, not by refining mental factors as are the *jhānas*, but by refining objects, by replacing a relatively gross object with a subtler one. The four attainments are named after their respective objects: the base of infinite space, the base of infinite consciousness, the base of nothingness, and the base of neither-perception-nor-non-perception.[5] These states represent levels of concentration so subtle and remote as to elude clear verbal explanation. The last of the four stands at the apex of mental concentration; it is the absolute, maximum degree of unification possible for consciousness. But even so, these absorptions reached by the path of serenity meditation, as exalted as they are, still lack the wisdom of insight, and so are not yet sufficient for gaining deliverance.

The kinds of concentration discussed so far arise by fixing the mind upon a single object to the exclusion of other objects. But apart from these there is another kind of concentration which does not depend upon restricting the range of awareness. This is called "momentary concentration" (*khaṇika-samādhi*). To develop momentary concentration the meditator does not deliberately attempt to exclude the multiplicity of phenomena from his field of attention. Instead, he simply directs mindfulness to the changing states of mind and body, noting any phenomenon that presents itself; the task is to maintain a continuous awareness of whatever enters the range of perception, clinging to nothing. As he goes on with his noting, concentration becomes stronger moment after moment until it becomes established one-pointedly on the constantly changing stream of events. Despite the change in the object, the mental unification remains steady, and in time acquires a force capable of suppressing the hindrances to a degree equal to that of access concentration. This fluid, mobile concentration is developed by the practice of the four foundations of mindfulness, taken up along the path of insight; when sufficiently strong it issues in the breakthrough to the last stage of the path, the arising of wisdom.

VIII

THE DEVELOPMENT
OF WISDOM

Though right concentration claims the last place among the factors of the Noble Eightfold Path, concentration itself does not mark the path's culmination. The attainment of concentration makes the mind still and steady, unifies its concomitants, opens vast vistas of bliss, serenity, and power. But by itself it does not suffice to reach the highest accomplishment, release from the bonds of suffering. To reach the end of suffering demands that the Eightfold Path be turned into an instrument of discovery, that it be used to generate the insights unveiling the ultimate truth of things. This requires the combined contributions of all eight factors, and thus a new mobilization of right view and right intention. Up to the present point these first two path factors have performed only a preliminary function. Now they have to be taken up again and raised to a higher level. Right view is to become a direct seeing into the real nature of phenomena, previously grasped only conceptually; right intention, to become a true renunciation of defilements born out of deep understanding.

Before we turn to the development of wisdom, it will be helpful to inquire why concentration is not adequate to the attainment of liberation. Concentration does not suffice to bring liberation because it fails to touch the defilements at their fundamental level. The Buddha teaches that the defilements are stratified into three layers: the stage of latent tendency, the stage of manifestation, and the stage of transgression. The most deeply grounded is the level of latent tendency (*anusaya*), where a defilement merely lies dormant without displaying any activity. The second level is the stage of manifestation (*pariyuṭṭhāna*), where a defilement, through the impact of some stimulus, surges up in the form of unwholesome thoughts, emotions, and volitions. Then, at the third level, the defilement passes beyond a purely mental manifestation to motivate some unwholesome action of body or speech. Hence this level is called the stage of transgression (*vītikkama*).

The three divisions of the Noble Eightfold Path provide the check against this threefold layering of the defilements. The first, the training in moral discipline, restrains unwholesome bodily and verbal activity and thus prevents defilements from reaching the stage of transgression. The training in concentration provides the safeguard against the stage of manifestation. It removes already manifest defilements and protects the mind from their continued influx. But even though concentration may be pursued to the depths of full absorption, it cannot touch the basic source of affliction—the latent tendencies lying dormant in the mental continuum. Against these concentration is powerless, since to root them out calls for more than mental calm. What it calls for, beyond the composure and serenity of the unified mind, is wisdom (*paññā*), a penetrating vision of phenomena in their fundamental mode of being.

Wisdom alone can cut off the latent tendencies at their root because the most fundamental member of the set, the one which nurtures the others and holds them in place, is ignorance (*avijjā*), and wisdom is the remedy for ignorance. Though verbally a negative, "unknowing," ignorance is not a factual negative, a mere privation of right knowledge. It is, rather, an insidious and volatile mental factor incessantly at work inserting itself into every compartment of our inner life. It distorts cognition, dominates volition, and determines the entire tone of our existence. As the Buddha says: "The element of ignorance is indeed a powerful element" (SN 14:13).

At the cognitive level, which is its most basic sphere of operation, ignorance infiltrates our perceptions, thoughts, and views, so that we come to misconstrue our experience, overlaying it with multiple strata of delusions. The most important of these delusions are three: the delusions of seeing permanence in the impermanent, of seeing satisfaction in the unsatisfactory, and of seeing a self in the selfless.[1] Thus we take ourselves and our world to be solid, stable, enduring entities, despite the ubiquitous reminders that everything is subject to change and destruction. We assume we have an innate right to pleasure, and direct our efforts to increasing and intensifying our enjoyment with an anticipatory fervour undaunted by repeated encounters with pain, disappointment, and frustration. And we perceive ourselves as self-contained egos, clinging to the various ideas and images we form of ourselves as the irrefragable truth of our identity.

Whereas ignorance obscures the true nature of things, wisdom removes the veils of distortion, enabling us to see phenomena in their fundamental mode of being with the vivacity of direct perception. The training in wisdom centres on the development of insight (*vipassanā-bhāvanā*), a deep and comprehensive seeing into the nature of existence which fathoms the truth of our being in the only sphere where it is directly accessible to us, namely, in our own experience. Normally we are immersed in our experience, identified with it so completely that we do not comprehend it. We live it but fail to understand its nature. Due to this blindness experience comes to be misconstrued, worked upon by the delusions of permanence, pleasure, and self. Of these cognitive distortions, the most deeply grounded and resistant is the delusion of self, the idea that at the core of our being there exists a truly established "I" with which we are essentially identified. This notion of self, the Buddha teaches, is an error, a mere presupposition lacking a real referent. Yet, though a mere presupposition, the idea of self is not inconsequential. To the contrary, it entails consequences that can be calamitous. Because we make the view of self the lookout point from which we survey the world, our minds divide everything up into the dualities of "I" and "not I," what is "mine" and what is "not mine." Then, trapped in these dichotomies, we fall victim to the defilements they breed, the urges to grasp and destroy, and finally to the suffering that inevitably follows.

To free ourselves from all defilements and suffering, the illusion of selfhood that sustains them has to be dispelled, exploded by the realization of selflessness. Precisely this is the task set for the development of wisdom. The first step along the path of development is an analytical one. In order to uproot the view of self, the field of experience has to be laid out in certain sets of factors, which are then methodically investigated to ascertain that none of them singly or in combination can be taken as a self. This analytical treatment of experience, so characteristic of the higher reaches of Buddhist philosophical psychology, is not intended to suggest that experience, like a watch or car, can be reduced to an accidental conglomeration of separable parts. Experience does have an irreducible unity, but this unity is functional rather than substantial; it does not require the postulate of a unifying self separate from the factors, retaining its identity as a constant amidst the ceaseless flux.

The method of analysis applied most often is that of the five aggregates of clinging (*pañc'upādānakkhandhā*): material form, feeling, perception, mental formations, and consciousness.[2] Material form constitutes the material side of existence: the bodily organism with its sense faculties and the outer objects of cognition. The other four aggregates constitute the mental side. Feeling provides the affective tone, perception the factor of noting and identifying, the mental formations the volitional and emotive elements, and consciousness the basic awareness essential to the whole occasion of experience. The analysis by way of the five aggregates paves the way for an attempt to see experience solely in terms of its constituting factors, without slipping in implicit references to an unfindable self. To gain this perspective requires the development of intensive mindfulness, now applied to the fourth foundation, the contemplation of the factors of existence (*dhammānupassanā*). The disciple will dwell contemplating the five aggregates, their arising and passing:

> The disciple dwells in contemplation of phenomena, namely, of the five aggregates of clinging. He knows what material form is, how it arises, how it passes away; knows what feeling is, how it arises, how it passes away; knows what perception is, how it arises, how it passes away; knows what mental formations are, how they arise, how they pass away; knows what consciousness is, how it arises, how it passes away.[3]

Or the disciple may instead base his contemplation on the six internal and external spheres of sense experience, that is, the six sense faculties and their corresponding objects, also taking note of the "fetters" or defilements that arise from such sensory contacts:

> The disciple dwells in contemplation of phenomena, namely, of the six internal and external sense bases. He knows the eye and forms, the ear and sounds, the nose and odours,

the tongue and tastes, the body and tangibles, the mind and mental objects; and he knows as well the fetter that arises in dependence on them. He understands how the unarisen fetter arises, how the arisen fetter is abandoned, and how the abandoned fetter does not arise again in the future.[4]

The view of self is further attenuated by examining the factors of existence, not analytically, but in terms of their relational structure. Inspection reveals that the aggregates exist solely in dependence on conditions. Nothing in the set enjoys the absolute self-sufficiency of being attributed to the assumed "I." Whatever factors in the body-mind complex be looked at, they are found to be dependently arisen, tied to the vast net of events extending beyond themselves temporally and spatially. The body, for example, has arisen through the union of sperm and egg and subsists in dependence on food, water, and air. Feeling, perception, and mental formations occur in dependence on the body with its sense faculties. They require an object, the corresponding consciousness, and the contact of the object with the consciousness through the media of the sense faculties. Consciousness in its turn depends on the sentient organism and the entire assemblage of co-arisen mental factors. This whole process of becoming, moreover, has arisen from the previous lives in this particular chain of existences and inherit all the accumulated *kamma* of the earlier existences. Thus nothing possesses a self-sufficient mode of being. All conditioned phenomena exist relationally, contingent and dependent on other things.

The above two steps—the factorial analysis and the discernment of relations—help cut away the intellectual adherence to the idea of self, but they lack sufficient power to destroy the ingrained clinging to the ego sustained by erroneous perception. To uproot this subtle form of ego-clinging requires a counteractive perception: direct insight into the empty, coreless nature of phenomena. Such an insight is generated by contemplating the factors of existence in terms of their three universal marks—impermanence (*aniccatā*), unsatisfactoriness (*dukkhatā*), and selflessness (*anattatā*). Generally, the first of the three marks to be discerned is impermanence, which at the level of insight does not mean merely that everything eventually comes to an end. At this level it means something deeper and more pervasive, namely, that conditioned phenomena are in constant process, happenings which break up and perish almost as soon as they arise. The stable objects appearing to the senses reveal themselves to be strings of momentary formations (*saṅkhārā*); the person posited by common sense dissolves into a current made up of two intertwining streams—a stream of material events, the aggregate of material form, and a stream of mental events, the other four aggregates.

When impermanence is seen, insight into the other two marks closely follows. Since the aggregates are constantly breaking up, we cannot pin our hopes on them for any lasting satisfaction. Whatever expectations we lay on them are bound to be dashed to pieces by their inevitable change. Thus when seen with insight they are *dukkha*, suffering, in the deepest sense. Then, as the aggregates are impermanent and unsatisfactory, they cannot be taken as self. If they were self, or the belongings of a self, we would be able to control them and bend them to our will, to make them everlasting sources of bliss. But far from being able to exercise such mastery, we find them to be grounds of pain and disappointment. Since they cannot be subjected to control, these very factors of our being are *anattā*: not a self, not the belongings of a self, just empty, ownerless phenomena occurring in dependence on conditions.

When the course of insight practice is entered, the eight path factors become charged with an intensity previously unknown. They gain in force and fuse together into the unity of a single cohesive path heading towards the goal. In the practice of insight all eight factors and three trainings co-exist; each is there supporting all the others; each makes its own unique contribution to the work. The factors of moral discipline hold the tendencies to transgression in check with such care that even the thought of unethical conduct does not arise. The factors of the concentration group keep the mind firmly fixed upon the stream of phenomena, contemplating whatever arises with impeccable precision, free from forgetfulness and distraction. Right view, as the wisdom of insight, grows continually sharper and deeper; right intention shows itself in a detachment and steadiness of purpose bringing an unruffled poise to the entire process of contemplation.

Insight meditation takes as its objective sphere the "conditioned formations" (*saṅkhārā*) comprised in the five aggregates. Its task is to uncover their essential characteristics: the three marks of impermanence, unsatisfactoriness, and selflessness. Because it still deals with the world of conditioned events, the Eightfold Path in the stage of insight is called the mundane path (*lokiyamagga*). This designation in no way implies that the path of insight is concerned with mundane goals, with achievements falling in the range of *saṃsāra*. It aspires to transcendence, it leads to liberation, but its objective domain of contemplation still lies within the conditioned world. However, this mundane contemplation of the conditioned serves as the vehicle for reaching the unconditioned, for attaining the supramundane. When insight meditation reaches its climax, when it fully comprehends the impermanence, unsatisfactoriness, and selflessness of everything formed, the mind breaks through the conditioned and realizes the unconditioned, Nibbāna. It sees Nibbāna with direct vision, makes it an object of immediate realization.

The breakthrough to the unconditioned is achieved by a type of consciousness or mental event called the supramundane path (*lokuttaramagga*). The supramundane path occurs in four stages, four "supramundane paths," each marking a deeper level of realization and issuing in a fuller degree of liberation, the fourth and last in complete liberation. The four paths can be achieved in close proximity to one another—for those with extraordinarily sharp faculties even in the same sitting—or (as is more typically the case) they can be spread out over time, even over several lifetimes.[5] The supramundane paths share in common the penetration of the Four Noble Truths. They understand them, not conceptually, but intuitively. They grasp them through vision, seeing them with self-validating certainty to be the invariable truths of existence. The vision of the truths which they present is complete at one moment. The four truths are not understood sequentially, as in the stage of reflection when thought is the instrument of understanding. They are seen simultaneously: to see one truth with the path is to see them all.

As the path penetrates the four truths, the mind exercises four simultaneous functions, one regarding each truth. It fully comprehends the truth of suffering, seeing all conditioned existence as stamped with the mark of unsatisfactoriness. At the same time it abandons craving, cuts through the mass of egotism and desire that repeatedly gives birth to suffering. Again, the mind realizes cessation, the deathless element Nibbāna, now directly present to the inner eye. And fourthly, the mind develops the Noble Eightfold Path, whose eight factors spring up endowed with tremendous power, attained to supramundane stature: right view as the direct seeing of Nibbāna, right intention as the mind's application to Nibbāna, the triad of ethical factors as the checks on moral transgression, right effort as the energy in the path-consciousness, right mindfulness as the factor of awareness, and right concentration as the mind's one-pointed focus. This ability of the mind to perform four functions at the same moment is compared to a candle's ability to simultaneously burn the wick, consume the wax, dispel darkness, and give light.[6]

The supramundane paths have the special task of eradicating the defilements. Prior to the attainment of the paths, in the stages of concentration and even insight meditation, the defilements were not cut off but were only debilitated, checked and suppressed by the training of the higher mental faculties. Beneath the surface they continued to linger in the form of latent tendencies. But when the supramundane paths are reached, the work of eradication begins.

Insofar as they bind us to the round of becoming, the defilements are classified into a set of ten "fetters" (*saṃyojana*) as follows: (1) personality view, (2) doubt, (3) clinging to rules and rituals, (4) sensual desire, (5) aversion, (6) desire for fine-material existence, (7) desire for immaterial existence, (8) conceit, (9) restlessness, and (10) ignorance. The four supramundane paths each eliminate a certain layer of defilements. The first, the path of stream-entry (*sotāpatti-magga*), cuts off the first three fetters, the coarsest of the set, eliminates them so they can never arise again. "Personality view" (*sakkāya-diṭṭhi*), the view of a truly existent self in the five aggregates, is cut off since one sees the selfless nature of all phenomena. Doubt is eliminated because one has grasped the truth proclaimed by the Buddha, seen it for oneself, and so can never again hang back due to uncertainty. And clinging to rules and rites is removed since one knows that deliverance can be won only through the practice of the Eightfold Path, not through rigid moralism or ceremonial observances.

The path is followed immediately by another state of supramundane consciousness known as the fruit (*phala*), which results from the path's work of cutting off defilements. Each path is followed by its own fruit, wherein for a few moments the mind enjoys the blissful peace of Nibbāna before descending again to the level of mundane consciousness. The first fruit is the fruit of stream-entry, and a person who has gone through the experience of this fruit becomes a "stream-enterer" (*sotāpanna*). He has entered the stream of the Dhamma carrying him to final deliverance. He is bound for liberation and can no longer fall back into the ways of an unenlightened worldling. He still has certain defilements remaining in his mental makeup, and it may take him as long as seven more lives to arrive at the final goal, but he has acquired the essential realization needed to reach it, and there is no way he can fall away.

An enthusiastic practitioner with sharp faculties, after reaching stream-entry, does not relax his striving but puts forth energy to complete the entire path as swiftly as possible. He resumes his practice of insight contemplation, passes through the ascending stages of insight-knowledge, and in time reaches the second path, the path of the once-returner (*sakadāgāmi-magga*). This supramundane path does not totally eradicate any of the fetters, but it attenuates the roots of greed, aversion, and delusion. Following the path the meditator experiences its fruit, then emerges as a "once-returner" who will return to this world at most only one more time before attaining full liberation.

But our practitioner again takes up the task of contemplation. At the next stage of supramundane realization he attains the third path, the path of the non-returner (*anāgāmi-magga*), with which he cuts off the two fetters of sensual desire and ill will. From that point on he can never again fall into the grip of any desire for sense pleasure, and can never be aroused to anger, aversion, or discontent. As a non-returner he will not return to the human state of existence in any future life. If he does not reach the last path in this very life, then after death he will be reborn in a higher sphere in the fine-material world (*rūpaloka*) and there reach deliverance.

But our meditator again puts forth effort, develops insight, and at its climax enters the fourth path, the path of arahatship (*arahatta-magga*). With this path he cuts off the five remaining fetters—desire for fine-material existence and desire for immaterial existence, conceit, restlessness, and ignorance. The first is the desire for rebirth into the celestial planes made accessible by the four *jhānas*, the planes commonly subsumed under the name "the Brahma-world." The second is the desire for rebirth into the four immaterial planes made accessible by the achievement of the four immaterial attainments. Conceit (*māna*) is not the coarse type of pride to which we become disposed through an over-estimation of our virtues and talents, but the subtle residue of the notion of an ego which subsists even after conceptually explicit views of self have been eradicated. The texts refer to this type of conceit as the conceit "I am" (*asmimāna*). Restlessness (*uddhacca*) is the subtle excitement which persists in any mind not yet completely enlightened, and ignorance (*avijjā*) is the fundamental cognitive obscuration which prevents full understanding of the Four Noble Truths. Although the grosser grades of ignorance have been scoured from the mind by the wisdom faculty in the first three paths, a thin veil of ignorance overlays the truths even in the non-returner.

The path of arahatship strips away this last veil of ignorance and, with it, all the residual mental defilements. This path issues in perfect comprehension of the Four Noble Truths. It fully fathoms the truth of suffering; eradicates the craving from which suffering springs; realizes with complete clarity the unconditioned element, Nibbāna, as the cessation of suffering; and consummates the development of the eight factors of the Noble Eightfold Path.

With the attainment of the fourth path and fruit the disciple emerges as an arahat, one who in this very life has been liberated from all bonds. The arahat has walked the Noble Eightfold Path to its end and lives in the assurance stated so often in the formula from the Pāli Canon: "Destroyed is birth; the holy life has been lived; what had to be done has been done; there is no coming back to any state of being." The arahat is no longer a practitioner of the path but its living embodiment. Having developed the eight factors of the path to their consummation, the Liberated One lives in the enjoyment of their fruits, enlightenment and final deliverance.

Epilogue

This completes our survey of the Noble Eightfold Path, the way to deliverance from suffering taught by the Buddha. The higher reaches of the path may seem remote from us in our present position, the demands of practice may appear difficult to fulfil. But even if the heights of realization are now distant, all that we need to reach them lies just beneath our feet. The eight factors of the path are always accessible to us; they are mental components which can be established in the mind simply through determination and effort. We have to begin by straightening out our views and clarifying our intentions. Then we have to purify our conduct—our speech, action, and livelihood. Taking these measures as our foundation, we have to apply ourselves with energy and mindfulness to the cultivation of concentration and insight. The rest is a matter of gradual practice and gradual progress, without expecting quick results. For some progress may be rapid, for others it may be slow, but the rate at which progress occurs should not cause elation or discouragement. Liberation is the inevitable fruit of the path and is bound to blossom forth when there is steady and persistent practice. The only requirements for reaching the final goal are two: to start and to continue. If these requirements are met there is no doubt the goal will be attained. This is the Dhamma, the undeviating law.

NOTES

CHAPTER I

1. Ignorance is actually identical in nature with the unwholesome root "delusion" (*moha*). When the Buddha speaks in a psychological context about mental factors, he generally uses the word "delusion"; when he speaks about the causal basis of *saṃsāra*, he uses the word "ignorance" (*avijjā*).
2. SN 56:11; Word of the Buddha, p. 26
3. Ibid.

CHAPTER II

1. *Adhisīlasikkhā, adhicittasikkhā, adhipaññāsikkhā.*
2. AN 3:33; Word of the Buddha, p. 19.
3. MN 117; Word of the Buddha, p. 36.
4. AN 6:63; Word of the Buddha, p. 19.
5. MN 9; Word of the Buddha, p. 29.
6. See DN 2, MN 27, etc. For details, see Vism. XIII, 72-101.
7. DN 22; Word of the Buddha, p. 29.
8. DN 22, SN 56:11; Word of the Buddha, p. 3
9. Ibid. Word of the Buddha, p. 16.
10. Ibid. Word of the Buddha, p. 22.

CHAPTER III

1. *Nekkhammasaṅkappa, abyāpāda saṅkappa, avihiṃsāsaṅkappa.*
2. *Kāmasaṅkappa, byāpādasaṅkappa, avihiṃsāsaṅkappa.* Though *kāma* usually means sensual desire, the context seems to allow a wider interpretation, as self-seeking desire in all its forms.
3. AN 1:16.2.
4. Strictly speaking, greed or desire (*rāga*) becomes immoral only when it impels actions violating the basic principles of ethics, such as killing, stealing, adultery, etc. When it remains merely as a mental factor or issues in actions not inherently immoral—e.g. the enjoyment of good food, the desire for recognition, sexual relations that do not

hurt others—it is not immoral but is still a form of craving causing
bondage to suffering.

5. For a full account of the *dukkha* tied up with sensual desire, see MN
   13.

6. This might appear to contradict what we said earlier, that mettā is
   free from self-reference. The contradiction is only apparent, however, for in developing mettā towards oneself one regards oneself
   objectively, as a third person. Further, the kind of love developed
   is not self-cherishing but a detached altruistic wish for one's own
   well-being.

7. Any other formula found to be effective may be used in place of the
   formula given here. For a full treatment, see Ñāṇamoli Thera, The
   Practice of Loving-kindness, Wheel No. 7.

CHAPTER IV

1. AN 10:176; Word of the Buddha, p. 50.

2. MN 61.

3. AN 10:176; Word of the Buddha, p. 50.

4. Subcommentary to Dīgha Nikāya.

5. AN 10:176; Word of the Buddha, pp. 50-51.

6. MN 21; Word of the Buddha, p. 51.

7. AN 10:176; Word of the Buddha, p. 51

8. AN 10:176; Word of the Buddha, p. 53.

9. HRH Prince Vajirañāṇavarorasa, The Five Precepts and the Five
   Ennoblers (Bangkok, 1975), pp. 1-9.

10. AN 10:176; Word of the Buddha, p. 53.

11. The Five Precepts and the Five Ennoblers gives a fuller list, pp. 10-13.

12. AN 10:176; Word of the Buddha, p. 53.

13. The following is summarized from The Five Precepts and the Five
    Ennoblers, pp. 16-18.

14. See AN 4:62; AN 5:41; AN 8:54.

15. The Five Precepts and the Five Ennoblers, pp. 45-47.

CHAPTER V

1. *Papañcasūdanī* (Commentary to Majjhima Nikāya).

2. MN 70; Word of the Buddha, pp. 59-60.

3. AN 4:13; Word of the Buddha, p. 57.

4. *Kāmacchanda, byāpāda, thīna-middha, uddhacca-kukkucca, vicikicchā.*

5. AN 4:14; Word of the Buddha, p. 57.

6. AN 4:13; Word of the Buddha, p. 58.

7. AN 4:14; Word of the Buddha, p. 58.

8. MN 20; Word of the Buddha, p. 58.

9. For a full treatment of the methods for dealing with the hindrances individually, consult the commentary to the Satipaṭṭhāna Sutta (DN 22, MN 10). A translation of the relevant passages, with further extracts from the subcommentary, can be found in Soma Thera, The Way of Mindfulness, pp. 116-26.

10. AN 4:13; Word of the Buddha, pp. 58-59.

11. AN 4:14; Word of the Buddha, p.59. The Pāli names for the seven are: *satisambojjhaṅga, dhammavicayasambojjhaṅga, viriyasambojjhaṅga, pītisambojjhaṅga, passaddhisambojjhaṅga, samādhisambojjhaṅga, upekkhāsambojjhaṅga.*

12. AN 4:13; Word of the Buddha, p. 59.

13. AN 4:14; Word of the Buddha, p. 59.

CHAPTER VI

1. *Dhammo sandiṭṭhiko akāliko ehipassiko opanayiko paccattaṃ veditabbo viññūhi.* (M. 7, etc.)

2. Commentary to Vism. See Vism. XIV, n. 64.

3. Sometimes the word satipaṭṭhāna is translated "foundation of mindfulness," with emphasis on the objective side, sometimes "application of mindfulness," with emphasis on the subjective side. Both explanations are allowed by the texts and commentaries.

4. DN 22; Word of the Buddha, p. 61.

5. Ibid. Word of the Buddha, p. 61.

6. For details, see Vism. VIII, 145-244.

7. See Soma Thera, The Way of Mindfulness, pp. 58-97.

8. *Asubha-bhāvanā.* The same subject is also called the perception of repulsiveness (*paṭikkūlasaññā*) and mindfulness concerning the body (*kāyagatā sati*).

9. For details, see Vism. VIII, 42-144.

10. For details, see Vism. XI, 27-117.

11. For a full account, see Soma Thera, The Way of Mindfulness, pp. 116-127.

12. Ibid., pp. 131-146.

CHAPTER VII

1. In what follows I have to restrict myself to a brief overview. For a full exposition, see Vism., Chapters III-XI.

2. See Vism. IV, 88-109.

3. Some common renderings such as "trance," "musing," etc., are altogether misleading and should be discarded.

4. DN 22; Word of the Buddha, pp. 80-81.

5. In Pāli: *ākāsānañcāyatana, viññāṇañcāyatana, ākiñcaññāyatana, n'eva-saññā-nāsaññāyatana.*

CHAPTER VIII

1. *Anicce niccavipallāsa, dukkhe sukhavipallāsa, anattani atta-vipallāsa.* AN 4:49.

2. In Pāli: *rūpakkhandha, vedanākkhandha, saññākkhandha, saṅkhārakkhandha, viññāṇakkhandha.*

3. DN 22; Word of the Buddha, pp. 71-72.

4. DN 22; Word of the Buddha, p. 73.

5. In the first edition of this book I stated here that the four paths have to be passed through sequentially, such that there is no attainment of a higher path without first having reached the paths below it. This certainly seems to be the position of the Commentaries. However, the Suttas sometimes show individuals proceeding directly from the stage of worldling to the third or even the fourth path and fruit. Though the commentator explains that they passed through each preceding path and fruit in rapid succession, the canonical texts themselves give no indication that this has transpired but suggest an immediate realization of the higher stages without the intermediate attainment of the lower stages.

6. See Vism. XXII, 92-103.

A Factorial Analysis of the Noble Eightfold Path (Pāli and English)

I. Sammā diṭṭhi

- dukkhe ñāṇa
- dukkhasamudaye ñāṇa
- dukkhanirodhe ñaṇa
- dukkhanirodhagāmini-paṭipadāya ñāṇa

Right view

- understanding suffering
- understanding its origin
- understanding its cessation
- understanding the way leading to its cessation

II. Sammā saṅkappa

- nekkhamma-saṅkappa
- abyāpāda-saṅkappa
- avihiṃsā-saṅkappa

Right intention

- intention of renunciation
- intention of good will
- intention of harmlessness

III. Sammā vācā

- musāvādā veramaṇī
- pisuṇāya vācāya veramaṇī
- pharusāya vācāya veramaṇi
- samphappalāpā veramaṇī

Right speech

- abstaining from false speech
- abstaining from slanderous speech
- abstaining from harsh speech
- abstaining from idle chatter

IV. Sammā kammanta

- pāṇātipātā veramaṇi
- adinnādānā veramaṇi
- kāmesu micchācārā veramaṇi

Right action

- abstaining from taking life
- abstaining from stealing
- abstaining from sexual misconduct

V. **Sammā ājīva**

- micchā ājīvaṃ pahāya sammā ājīvena jīvitaṃ kappeti

Right livelihood

- giving up wrong livelihood one earns one's living by right forms of livelihood

VI. **Sammā vāyāma**

- saṃvarappadhāna
- pahānappadhāna
- bhāvanāppadhāna

- anurakkhaṇappadhāna

Right effort

- the effort to restrain defilements

- the effort to abandon defilements

- the effort to develop wholesome states

- the effort to maintain wholesome states

VII. **Sammā sati**

- kāyānupassanā

- vedanānupassanā

- cittānupassanā

- dhammānupassanā

Right mindfulness

- mindful contemplation of the body

- mindful contemplation of feeling

- mindful contemplation of the mind

- mindful contemplation of phenomena

VIII. **Sammā samādhi**

- paṭhamajjhāna
- dutiyajjhāna
- tatiyajjhāna
- catutthajjhāna

Right concentration

- the first *jhāna*
- the second *jhāna*
- the third *jhāna*
- the fourth *jhāna*

RECOMMENDED READINGS

I. General treatments of the Noble Eightfold Path
    Ledi Sayadaw. *The Noble Eightfold Path and Its Factors Explained.*
        (Wheel 245/247).
    Nyanatiloka Thera. *The Word of the Buddha.*
        (BPS 14th ed., 1968).
    Piyadassi Thera. *The Buddha's Ancient Path.*
        (BPS 3rd ed., 1979).

II. Right View
    Ñāṇamoli, Bhikkhu. *The Discourse on Right View.*
        (Wheel 377/379).
    Nyanatiloka Thera. *Karma and Rebirth.* (Wheel 9).
    Story, Francis. *The Four Noble Truths.* (Wheel 34/35).
    Wijesekera, O.H. de A. *The Three Signata.* (Wheel 20).

III. Right Intentions
    Ñāṇamoli Thera. *The Practice of Lovingkindness.* (Wheel 7).
    Nyanaponika Thera. *The Four Sublime States.* (Wheel 6).
    Prince, T. *Renunciation.* (Bodhi Leaf B 36).

IV. Right Speech, Right Action, & Right Livelihood
    Bodhi, Bhikkhu. *Going for Refuge and Taking the Precepts.* (Wheel
        282/284).
    Narada Thera. *Everyman's Ethics.* (Wheel 14).
    Vajirañāṇavarorasa. *The Five Precepts and the Five Ennoblers.*
        (Bangkok: Mahāmakuṭa, 1975).

V. Right Effort
    Nyanaponika Thera. *The Five Mental Hindrances and Their Con-
        quest.* (Wheel 26).
    Piyadassi Thera. *The Seven Factors of Enlightenment.* (Wheel 1).
    Soma Thera. *The Removal of Distracting Thoughts.* (Wheel 21).

VI. Right Mindfulness

Nyanaponika Thera. *The Heart of Buddhist Meditation.* (London: Rider, 1962; BPS, 1992).

Nyanaponika Thera. *The Power of Mindfulness.* (Wheel 121/122).

Nyanasatta Thera. *The Foundations of Mindfulness* (*Satipaṭṭhāna Sutta*). (Wheel 19).

Soma Thera. *The Way of Mindfulness.* (BPS, 3rd ed., 1967).

VII. Right Concentration & The Development of Wisdom

Buddhaghosa, Bhadantacariya. *The Path of Purification* (*Visuddhimagga*).Translated by Bhikkhu Ñāṇamoli, 4th ed. (BPS, 1979).

Khantipālo, Bhikkhu. *Calm and Insight.* (London: Curzon, 1980).

Ledi Sayadaw. *A Manual of Insight.* (Wheel 31/32).

Nyanatiloka Thera. *The Buddha's Path to Deliverance.* (BPS, 1982).

Solé-Leris, Amadeo. *Tranquillity and Insight.* (London: Rider, 1986; BPS 1992).

Vajirañāṇa, Paravahera. *Buddhist Meditation in Theory and Practice.* 2nd ed. (Kuala Lumpur, Malaysia: Buddhist Missionary Society, 1975).

All BPS books, Wheel, and Bodhi Leaf publications referred to above are published by the Buddhist Publication Society, and are available in the Americas from Pariyatti (www.pariyatti.org).

ABOUT PARIYATTI

Pariyatti is dedicated to providing affordable access to authentic teachings of the Buddha about the Dhamma theory (*pariyatti*) and practice (*paṭipatti*) of Vipassana meditation. A 501(c)(3) nonprofit charitable organization since 2002, Pariyatti is sustained by contributions from individuals who appreciate and want to share the incalculable value of the Dhamma teachings. We invite you to visit www.pariyatti.org to learn about our programs, services, and ways to support publishing and other undertakings.

Pariyatti Publishing Imprints

Vipassana Research Publications (focus on Vipassana as taught by S.N. Goenka in the tradition of Sayagyi U Ba Khin)

BPS Pariyatti Editions (selected titles from the Buddhist Publication Society, copublished by Pariyatti in the Americas)

Pariyatti Digital Editions (audio and video titles, including discourses)

Pariyatti Press (classic titles returned to print and inspirational writing by contemporary authors)

Pariyatti enriches the world by

- disseminating the words of the Buddha,
- providing sustenance for the seeker's journey,
- illuminating the meditator's path.